The
TWENTY-
MINUTE
ONE-DISH
GOURMET

For Julie & Steve,

Happy Holidays!

Karen A. Levin

11-'96

The
TWENTY-MINUTE ONE-DISH GOURMET

Delicious, Easy-to-Make
Meals That Everyone Will Love

Karen A. Levin

CONTEMPORARY BOOKS
A TRIBUNE COMPANY

Library of Congress Cataloging-in-Publication Data

Levin, Karen A.
    The twenty-minute one-dish gourmet : delicious, easy-to-make
meals that everyone will love / Karen A. Levin.
       p.   cm.
    Includes index.
    ISBN 0-8092-3198-0
    1. Entrées (Cookery)   2. Quick and easy cookery.   I. Title.
TX740.L483   1996
641.5′55—dc20   96-4087
                                                         CIP

Cover design by Kim Bartko
Cover photo by John Morrison
Interior design by Mary Lockwood

Featured on the cover: Cajun Chicken Breasts with Aromatic Rice
(see Index)

Published by Contemporary Books
An imprint of NTC/Contemporary Publishing Company
Two Prudential Plaza, Chicago, Illinois 60601-6790
Manufactured in the United States of America
International Standard Book Number: 0-8092-3198-0
10   9   8   7   6   5   4   3   2   1

To my talented, loving children,
Amelia and Andrew,
whose support, encouragement, and willingness to try everything
has made this book a labor of love

Contents

5. HOT AND HEARTY SANDWICHES   79

6. MAIN DISH SALADS   103

Introduction

It seems as though we Americans want our meals on the table faster than ever before. Nearly all supermarkets these days have a deli section full of take-out foods that only need reheating. Restaurants are enjoying a surge in patrons, especially those who call ahead and pick up the food to bring home. The key word here is *home*. "Cocooning," a relatively new term that describes the trend of Americans longing for the comforts of the home environment, is bigger than ever. The problem is that although many of us have limited time and energy to prepare a home-cooked meal, we want to eat at home. Unfortunately, we've also grown tired of reheated, expensive food from the market as our main source of dinner. Men/women/children cannot live on roasted chicken and mostaccioli alone. The solution to our dining dilemma may well harken the next trend, now called "Speed Scratch"—using the many convenience products that savvy food manufacturers have provided for us to create quick meals. This method is a step in the right direction, but, of course, it still takes a reasonable amount of creativity to make those meals exciting, varied, and healthy.

This cookbook is designed to answer that challenge. All of the meals in *The Twenty-Minute One-Dish Gourmet* are delicious, attractive, well-balanced, and can be prepared in twenty minutes or less from start to finish. The recipes in this book are more than just main dish entrees; these meals contain a balance of vegetables, protein, and carbohydrates. As with many one-dish meals, a salad or bread may be desired to round out the meal and add temperature contrast, so a simple serving suggestion is included with each recipe. The bonus is that there will be only *one* pot, skillet, or broiler pan to wash afterward.

The key to successful quick-cooking meals is planning and having a well-stocked cupboard. When you have time on the weekend, decide which recipes you will be preparing during the week and purchase as many of the ingredients as possible ahead of time. Of course, occasionally there will be a need for the brief stop to the market on your way home from work to pick up fresh produce, fish, or meat, but that shopping time will be kept to a minimum if the staple ingredients are already on hand. Chopping time can be saved by picking up onions, peppers, celery, and so on, at the supermarket salad bar. Careful reading of the recipe and assembling all the ingredients before you begin will ensure effortless preparation.

This book will convince you that it is indeed possible to dine well on quick, easy, less expensive, well-balanced, creative meals prepared at home. Enjoy.

The
TWENTY-
MINUTE
ONE-DISH
GOURMET

1

Skillet Meals

You will find a variety of delicious easy-to-make poultry, meat, fish, and meatless meals in this chapter. Their common thread is that they are all prepared in the most frequently used cooking pan in everyone's kitchen—the skillet. Because these dishes provide a complete meal, the amount of food that will be in your skillet is substantial. To ensure adequate cooking space, it is important that you use a large, deep skillet when a recipe specifically calls for a "deep" pan. This could be a sauté pan (or what our parents used to refer to as a "chicken frier"), about 10 inches in diameter and at least 2½ inches deep. If the recipe does not indicate "deep," you may use a sloped side 10-inch skillet. You will usually need a cover for the skillet in order to get the food quickly to a simmering temperature. Occasionally a nonstick skillet will be recommended for recipes such as egg dishes to keep foods from sticking without adding additional fat. Many of the recipes are already low in fat (especially considering that each recipe is a complete meal) but if you are on a *very* low fat diet, use a nonstick pan coated with nonstick vegetable spray and omit or decrease the fat called for in the recipe.

DILLED RED SNAPPER WITH PEAS AND COUSCOUS

MAKES 4 SERVINGS

While the fish is sautéing to a luscious golden brown, measure out the peas and couscous.

> 2 tablespoons all-purpose flour
> 1 teaspoon dried dill weed, divided
> ½ teaspoon salt
> ½ teaspoon Hungarian sweet paprika
> 2 tablespoons butter
> 1 tablespoon vegetable oil
> 4 4-ounce skinned red snapper fillets*
> 1 14½-ounce can chicken or vegetable broth
> 1 cup frozen peas
> 1 cup uncooked couscous
> Lemon wedges for garnish

Combine flour, ½ teaspoon dill weed, salt, and paprika in a shallow bowl or plate. Heat butter and oil in a large deep skillet over medium-high heat. Rinse fish with cold water; shake off excess water. Dip fish in flour mixture, turning to coat lightly. Sauté fish in butter mixture until golden brown, about 3 minutes per side. Transfer fish to a plate and set aside.

Combine broth and peas in the same skillet and bring to a boil over high heat. Stir in couscous and remaining ½ teaspoon dill weed. Place fish over couscous mixture. Cover and turn off heat under skillet. Let stand for 5 minutes or until liquid is absorbed and fish is opaque. Garnish with lemon wedges.

Serving suggestion: Serve with coleslaw.

If desired, you may substitute any skinned, firm, white-flesh fish such as halibut, scrod, or orange roughy for the red snapper.

SHRIMP AND PORCINI MUSHROOMS
WITH BROWN RICE

MAKES 4 SERVINGS

Dried mushrooms give this dish a wonderful rich flavor. The typical, time-consuming method of rehydrating the mushrooms by soaking them in water is eliminated in this easy one-dish meal. Purchase frozen cooked shrimp or cooked cocktail shrimp from the seafood section of your supermarket. If desired, you may substitute one 6½-ounce can lump crab meat (drained) for the shrimp.

> 1 tablespoon butter or margarine
> 1 teaspoon bottled minced garlic
> 1 14½-ounce can beef broth
> 1 cup water
> ½ ounce dried porcini mushrooms
> 1½ cups uncooked quick-cooking brown rice
> 8 ounces cooked, peeled, and deveined medium
>   shrimp
> 1 cup (4 ounces) freshly grated Asiago or
>   Parmesan cheese
> Freshly ground black pepper (optional)

Melt butter in a large deep skillet over medium-high heat. Add garlic and cook for 1 minute. Add broth and water. Using kitchen shears, quickly cut mushrooms into small pieces and add to skillet as the mixture comes to a boil. Stir in rice. Cover, reduce heat, and simmer for 12 minutes or until mushrooms and rice are tender. Stir in shrimp and heat through. Remove from heat. Stir in cheese. Sprinkle with pepper, if desired.

Serving suggestion: Serve with a tossed green salad.

CAJUN CHICKEN BREASTS WITH AROMATIC RICE

MAKES 4 SERVINGS

Jasmine, basmati, wild pecan, and popcorn rice are among the "aromatic" rices of the world. They release a wonderful aroma while cooking and have a tempting nutty flavor. Look for them in the rice or ethnic section of your supermarket or specialty food stores. If they are unavailable, regular long-grain white rice may be substituted.

    1 14½-ounce can chicken broth
    1 cup aromatic rice such as popcorn, basmati, or
       jasmine
    4 4-ounce skinless, boneless chicken breast halves
    1 tablespoon blackened, Cajun, or Creole
       seasoning mix
    2 cups broccoli florets
    ½ cup chopped red and/or yellow bell peppers
    3 scallions

Combine broth and rice in a large deep skillet. Cover and bring to a boil over high heat. Reduce heat and simmer, covered for 5 minutes.

Meanwhile, place chicken breast halves between sheets of waxed paper or plastic wrap; pound to ½-inch thickness. Rub seasoning mix over both sides of chicken. Stir broccoli and bell pepper into rice mixture. Arrange chicken over rice mixture. Cover and simmer for 10 minutes or until chicken is cooked through and liquid is absorbed.

While chicken and rice are simmering, thinly slice scallions. Transfer chicken to serving plates. Stir scallions into the rice mixture and serve alongside chicken.

Serving suggestion: Serve with garlic bread.

CHICKEN WITH BARLEY PRIMAVERA

MAKES 4 SERVINGS

If you are watching your sodium intake, use low-sodium chicken broth and reduce the pesto to 2 tablespoons.

>   2 tablespoons butter or olive oil
>   1 pound chicken tenders or chicken or turkey
>   breast, cut for stir-fry
>   1 teaspoon Hungarian sweet paprika
>   ½ teaspoon salt
>   1 teaspoon bottled minced garlic
>   1 14½-ounce can chicken or vegetable broth
>   ¾ cup uncooked quick-cooking pearl barley
>   1 16-ounce package frozen mixed vegetable
>   medley such as broccoli, carrots, red bell
>   peppers, and onions
>   ¼ cup prepared pesto sauce

Heat butter in a large deep skillet over medium-high heat. Add chicken to skillet; sprinkle with paprika and salt. Add garlic and cook for 3 minutes, stirring occasionally. Transfer mixture to a plate or bowl and set aside. Add broth and barley to skillet. Cover and bring to a boil over high heat. Reduce heat and simmer for 7 minutes.

Meanwhile, thaw vegetables in a microwave oven on HIGH for 2 to 3 minutes or in a colander under warm running water. Stir thawed vegetables and reserved chicken mixture into barley mixture. Cover and simmer over medium-high heat for 4 to 5 minutes or until barley and vegetables are tender and chicken is cooked through. Stir in pesto and heat through.

Serving suggestion: Serve with crusty rye rolls.

MIDDLE EASTERN SKILLET DINNER

MAKES 4 SERVINGS

Look for packages of shredded carrot or broccoli "slaw" in your super-market's produce section.

1 tablespoon butter or margarine
1 cup chopped onion (frozen or fresh)
2 cups packaged shredded carrots or broccoli
   stems
1 teaspoon bottled minced garlic
8 ounces chicken or turkey breast, cut for stir-fry
8 ounces fully cooked kielbasa or smoked sausage
1 14½-ounce can vegetable or chicken broth
1 16-ounce can chickpeas (garbanzo beans),
   drained
¼ teaspoon turmeric
⅛ teaspoon cayenne pepper *or* ¼ teaspoon hot
   pepper sauce
1 cup uncooked couscous
Plain yogurt (optional)

Melt butter in a large deep skillet over medium-high heat. Add onion, carrots, and garlic and cook for 3 minutes, stirring occasionally. Add chicken and cook for 2 minutes.

Meanwhile, thinly slice sausage and stir into chicken mixture. Cook for 3 minutes or until chicken is cooked through, stirring occasionally. Add broth, chickpeas, turmeric, and cayenne pepper. Cover and bring to a boil over high heat. Stir in couscous. Turn off heat under skillet. Let stand, covered, for 5 minutes or until liquid is absorbed. Serve with yogurt, if desired.

🕐 *Serving suggestion:* Serve with warm pita bread.

Couscous Paella

Purchase colorful chopped bell peppers from your supermarket salad bar. If you frequent gourmet or specialty food stores, look for a variety of fully cooked sausages that will freeze well. Andouille, a fairly spicy sausage, is perfect for this quick paella.

1 tablespoon garlic-infused olive oil *or*
    1 tablespoon olive oil plus ½ teaspoon bottled
    minced garlic
1 cup chopped onion (frozen or fresh)
1 cup diced red, yellow, and/or green bell peppers
8 ounces fully cooked smoked sausage, cut into
    ½-inch-thick slices
1 14½-ounce can vegetable or chicken broth
¾ cup frozen peas
½ teaspoon crushed saffron threads *or*
    ¼ teaspoon ground saffron *or* ½ teaspoon
    turmeric
⅛ teaspoon cayenne pepper
8 ounces cooked, peeled, and deveined medium
    shrimp, thawed if frozen
1 14½-ounce can diced tomatoes, drained
1 cup uncooked couscous

Heat oil in a large deep skillet over medium-high heat. Add onion and bell pepper and cook for 4 minutes, stirring occasionally. Add sausage and cook for 1 minute more. Stir in broth, peas, saffron, and cayenne pepper. Bring to a boil over high heat. Stir in shrimp and tomatoes and return to a boil. Stir in couscous, mixing well. Cover; turn off heat under skillet. Let stand for 5 minutes or until liquid is absorbed.

🕐 *Serving suggestion:* Serve with warm pita bread or focaccia bread.

STEAK DIANE WITH ASPARAGUS AND MUSHROOMS

MAKES 4 SERVINGS

This elegant dish is perfect for entertaining because you will be able to spend more time with your guests. Cooked according to the directions, the steaks will be medium-rare. If you prefer medium or medium-well steaks, cook in the sauce an additional 2 to 4 minutes.

> 4 tablespoons butter, divided
> 4 4- to 5-ounce beef tenderloin steaks, cut 1 inch
>   thick
> Freshly ground black pepper
> 2 tablespoons Worcestershire sauce
> 2 tablespoons Dijon mustard
> 8 ounces fresh asparagus, cut into 1-inch pieces
> ¾ cup chopped red onion
> 2 3½- or 4-ounce packages mixed exotic
>   mushrooms *or* 1 package shiitake plus
>   1 package oyster mushrooms
> ⅔ cup whipping cream or half-and-half
> ¾ teaspoon dried thyme leaves
> 4 slices sourdough bread, toasted

Melt 2 tablespoons butter in a large deep skillet over medium-high heat. Sprinkle steaks lightly with pepper and add to skillet. Cook for 2 minutes per side. Reduce heat to medium; continue cooking steaks for 3 minutes more, turning once.

Transfer steaks to a plate; sprinkle with Worcestershire sauce and spread with mustard. Melt remaining 2 tablespoons butter in the same skillet. Add asparagus and onion and cook for 3 minutes, stirring occasionally. While asparagus mixture is cooking, rinse mushrooms and pat dry with a paper towel. (If using shiitake and oyster mushrooms, discard stems from shiitake mushrooms and thickly slice caps; halve large oyster mushrooms.) Add mushrooms to skillet and cook for 5 minutes, stirring occasionally. Add cream and thyme and cook for 1 minute more.

Return steaks and accumulated juices from plate to skillet. Cook until steaks are heated through, about 2 minutes, turning once. Serve steaks over toast. Top with mushroom-asparagus sauce.

Serving suggestion: Serve with mixed bitter greens tossed with a vinaigrette dressing.

SHEPHERD'S PIE

MAKES 4 SERVINGS

If your skillet is not ovenproof, wrap a double thickness of aluminum foil around the handle.

> 11 ounces frozen mashed potatoes (½ of a
>   22-ounce package)
> 1⅓ cups milk
> 1 pound lean ground beef
> 1 teaspoon bottled minced garlic
> 1 teaspoon dried thyme leaves
> ½ teaspoon salt
> ½ teaspoon freshly ground black pepper
> 1 12-ounce jar beef gravy with mushrooms
> 1 cup frozen peas
> ½ cup (2 ounces) shredded cheddar cheese

Preheat broiler. Prepare potatoes with milk for 4 servings in a microwave oven according to package directions. Meanwhile, cook beef, garlic, thyme, salt, and pepper in a 10-inch ovenproof skillet over medium-high heat until meat is no longer pink, stirring occasionally. Pour off drippings. Add gravy and peas and cook until peas are defrosted and mixture is very hot, about 3 minutes.

Spoon prepared mashed potatoes over meat mixture, spreading evenly and leaving a 1-inch border around edges. Sprinkle cheese evenly over potatoes. Place the skillet under the broiler and broil 4 to 5 inches from heat source for 2 to 3 minutes or until cheese is melted and mixture is bubbly.

Serving suggestion: Serve with a tossed green salad.

CORNED BEEF AND CABBAGE WITH HORSERADISH SAUCE

MAKES 4 SERVINGS

Packages of shredded coleslaw mix (which usually contain green and red cabbage and carrots) make this skillet meal a snap. Look for them in your supermarket produce section. Save the remaining broth in the skillet to add to soups or stews.

> 1 14½-ounce can vegetable broth
> 1 pound red potatoes, cut into 1-inch chunks
> ¼ cup light or regular mayonnaise
> 1 tablespoon Dijon mustard
> 1 tablespoon prepared horseradish
> 1 16-ounce package coleslaw mix
> 12 ounces sliced deli corned beef

Combine broth and potatoes in a large, deep skillet. Cover and bring to a boil over high heat. Reduce heat to medium and continue cooking, covered for 5 minutes. Meanwhile, combine mayonnaise, mustard, and horseradish in a small bowl and set aside.

Add coleslaw mix to skillet. Mix well (skillet will be full but mixture will shrink as it cooks). Cover and cook for 5 minutes. Stir mixture. Arrange corned beef slices in a single layer over vegetables in the skillet. Cover; turn off heat. Let stand for 5 minutes or until corned beef is hot. Transfer corned beef and vegetables with slotted spoon to serving plates and serve with horseradish sauce.

☺ *Serving suggestion:* Serve with caraway rye bread.

CORNED BEEF HASH WITH BASTED EGGS

MAKES 4 SERVINGS

The optional half-and-half is the trick restaurant chefs use to enrich this delicious hash. Steaming or "basting" the eggs eliminates having to poach or fry the eggs in a separate pan. There is room in the skillet for five eggs if someone would like two!

> 4 cups (16 ounces) frozen hash brown potatoes
>   with peppers and onions (O'Brien style)
> 2 tablespoons butter or margarine
> 8 ounces sliced deli corned beef
> 1 tablespoon prepared horseradish
> ¼ cup half-and-half or cream (optional)
> 4 large eggs
> Salt
> Freshly ground black pepper

Thaw potatoes in a microwave oven on HIGH for about 3 minutes. Meanwhile, melt butter in a large, deep nonstick skillet over medium-high heat. Add potatoes and cook for 7 minutes or until potatoes begin to brown, stirring occasionally.

Meanwhile, finely chop corned beef. Stir corned beef and horse-radish into potato mixture. Cook for 2 minutes, stirring occasionally. Stir in half and half, if desired. With the back of a large spoon, make four indentations in potato mixture. Break one egg into each indentation. Sprinkle eggs lightly with salt and pepper. Cover skillet; cook over medium-low heat for 3 to 4 minutes or until eggs are basted "easy" or 5 minutes for more well-done eggs.

🕐 *Serving suggestion:* Serve with applesauce and rye toast. Pass ketchup or chili sauce as a condiment for the potatoes.

Lamb Chops with Curried Couscous and Vegetables

MAKES 2 SERVINGS

If frozen bell pepper and onion strips are not available, substitute a frozen mixed vegetable medley such as broccoli, carrots, and cauliflower.

> 8 ounces frozen bell pepper and onion strips for
>   stir-fry
> 4 5- to 6-ounce well-trimmed loin lamb chops,
>   cut 1 inch thick
> ½ teaspoon garlic salt
> ¼ teaspoon freshly ground black pepper
> ¾ cup canned chicken or vegetable broth
> ¾ teaspoon curry powder
> ⅛ teaspoon cayenne pepper (optional)
> ½ cup uncooked couscous
> Prepared mango chutney or mint jelly (optional)

Thaw vegetables in a microwave oven on HIGH for about 2 minutes or in a colander under warm running water. Meanwhile, sprinkle lamb chops with garlic salt and pepper. Heat a large deep skillet over medium-high heat. Add lamb chops and cook for 3 minutes per side. Transfer chops to a plate and set aside.

Combine broth, thawed vegetables, curry powder, and cayenne pepper in the same skillet and bring to a boil. Stir in couscous; mix well. Return chops to skillet. Cover and turn off heat under skillet. Let stand for 5 minutes or until liquid is absorbed. Serve with chutney or mint jelly, if desired.

Serving suggestion: Serve with melon wedges.

PORK CHOPS WITH BAKED BEANS AND PEPPERS

MAKES 2 SERVINGS

A tasty, quick weeknight meal for two! Choose colorful, mixed, diced bell peppers from your supermarket salad bar.

> Nonstick vegetable spray
> 2 6-ounce well-trimmed center-cut loin pork
>   chops, cut ¾ inch thick
> 1 cup diced red, yellow, and/or green bell
>   peppers
> ⅓ cup diced red or yellow onion
> 1 teaspoon blackened, Cajun, or Creole
>   seasoning mix
> 1 16-ounce can *or* 1 18-ounce jar baked beans,
>   undrained

Coat a large nonstick skillet with nonstick vegetable spray. Heat over medium-high heat until hot. Add chops, bell peppers, and onion. Sprinkle evenly with seasoning mix and cook for 5 minutes. Turn chops, stir vegetable mixture, and continue cooking for 5 more minutes. Add beans to skillet and stir into vegetable mixture. Continue to cook for 4 to 5 minutes or until chops are no longer pink in center, stirring occasionally.

Serving suggestion: Serve with a Caesar salad.

POLENTA WITH SPICY SAUSAGE MARINARA SAUCE

MAKES 4 SERVINGS

Look for prepared chilled polenta next to the refrigerated pasta, or shelf-stable polenta (cornmeal mush) near the dried pasta. After slicing the polenta for this recipe, refrigerate the remainder for up to one week for use in other recipes or as an accompaniment to bacon or sausage.

To turn this recipe into a meatless meal, sauté 2 cups (about ½ pound) sliced crimini or other mushrooms in 1 tablespoon olive oil as a substitute for the sausage, and add one 6-ounce jar drained marinated artichoke hearts with the marinara sauce.

1 tablespoon garlic-infused or extra virgin olive oil
8 ½-inch thick slices prepared polenta or cornmeal mush
8 ounces hot Italian sausage, casings removed*
2 cups prepared marinara sauce or mushroom spaghetti sauce
¼ cup grated Parmesan, Romano, or Asiago cheese

Preheat oven to 200°F. Heat oil in a large skillet over medium heat. Add polenta slices and cook for 2 minutes per side or until heated through. Transfer polenta to four dinner plates and place in oven to keep warm while making sauce.

Cook sausage in the same skillet for 5 minutes or until no longer pink, stirring often to break sausage into small pieces. Pour off drippings. Add marinara sauce and heat through for about 5 minutes, stirring occasionally. Using a pot holder, remove plates from oven. Spoon sauce evenly over polenta; sprinkle with cheese.

☺ *Serving suggestion:* Serve with crusty Italian or French bread.

Fully cooked chicken Italian sausage may be substituted. Cut sausage in ¼-inch-thick slices; reduce sausage cooking time to 2 minutes.

SAUSAGES WITH SKILLET CORNCAKES

MAKES 3 TO 4 SERVINGS

Serve this New England–style brunch dish any time of day. If you have a freestanding electric griddle or a griddle on your range top, place the sausages to one side to cook while the corncakes are cooking on the other and omit the oven heating step. The syrup is easily warmed in a glass measuring cup or microwaveable pitcher in the microwave oven.

> 1 8-ounce package fully cooked brown-and-serve
>   sausages
> ¾ cup all-purpose flour
> ¼ cup cornmeal
> 2 tablespoons sugar
> 1 teaspoon baking powder
> ½ cup milk
> 1 large egg
> 2 tablespoons vegetable oil
> ½ cup (2 ounces) shredded cheddar cheese,
>   preferably sharp
> Pure maple syrup, heated if desired

Preheat oven to 200°F. Place sausages in a large nonstick skillet and cook over medium heat for 4 minutes. Turn and continue to cook for 3 minutes more or until browned and heated through.

Meanwhile, combine flour, cornmeal, sugar, and baking powder in a medium bowl. Add milk, egg, and oil, mixing with a fork just until dry ingredients are moistened. Stir in cheese and set aside. Transfer cooked sausages to four dinner plates. Place plates in oven to keep warm while preparing corncakes.

Wipe out the skillet with a paper towel and place over medium heat. Drop batter by scant ¼ cupfuls (in batches) into hot skillet. Cook for 1 to 2 minutes per side or until golden brown. Transfer corncakes as they are made to plates in oven; continue making corncakes with remaining batter. Using a pot holder, remove plates from the oven. Serve with syrup.

🕐 *Serving suggestion:* Serve with chunky cinnamon applesauce.

HOPPIN' JOHN

MAKES 3 TO 4 SERVINGS

This traditional Southern dish is typically served on New Year's day to bring to all who enjoy it good luck throughout the year. See if it brings you good luck on any of the other 364 days you choose to try it! If you cannot find canned black-eyed peas, substitute canned red or pink beans.

3 thick slices bacon, preferably apple wood
smoked, cut crosswise into ¼-inch pieces
1 small onion, chopped
1 teaspoon bottled minced garlic
1 cup quick-cooking brown rice
1 14½-ounce can vegetable broth
½ teaspoon hot pepper sauce
1 16-ounce can black-eyed peas, drained
1 large tomato, seeded and diced
1 cup (4 ounces) shredded sharp cheddar cheese

Cook bacon in a large deep skillet over medium-high heat for 2 minutes, stirring occasionally. Add onion and garlic to skillet and cook for 2 minutes more. Add rice; mix well. Stir in broth and pepper sauce. Cover and bring to a boil over high heat. Stir in black-eyed peas. Cover and simmer over medium-low heat for 10 minutes or until most of the liquid is absorbed. Stir in tomato. Transfer to four serving plates. Sprinkle with cheese.

Serving suggestion: Serve with a spinach salad.

Huevos Rancheros con Frijoles

MAKES 2 SERVINGS

Instead of turning the eggs over, you may baste them by covering the pan after the eggs are added. Look for bottles of hot ketchup or ketchup with jalapeño peppers next to the regular ketchup or substitute regular ketchup and add a healthy dash of hot pepper sauce.

¼ cup vegetable oil
2 7- to 8-inch corn or flour tortillas
½ cup chopped onion (frozen or fresh)
½ cup chopped green or red bell pepper
1 teaspoon bottled minced garlic
2 large eggs
1 8-ounce can kidney beans, drained
½ cup chunky salsa
2 tablespoons hot ketchup
¼ cup (1 ounce) shredded cheddar or cojack
    cheese
Chopped cilantro (optional)

Heat oil in a large skillet over medium-high heat until hot but not smoking. Fry tortillas one at a time in oil until lightly browned and crisp, about 1 minute per side. Transfer to paper towels to drain.

Carefully pour off all but 2 tablespoons oil. Reduce heat under skillet to medium-low. Add onion, bell pepper, and garlic to skillet and cook for 5 minutes over medium heat. Push vegetables to edges of skillet. Break eggs into center of skillet. Cook sunny-side up or over-easy, as desired. Transfer tortillas to two serving plates and top each with an egg. Add beans, salsa, and hot ketchup to skillet and heat through, stirring constantly. Spoon mixture over eggs. Top with cheese. Sprinkle with cilantro, if desired.

☺ *Serving suggestion:* Serve with a fresh fruit salad.

Goat Cheese Omelet with Hash Brown Potatoes

MAKES 2 SERVINGS

Purchase goat cheese (chèvre) in 4-ounce logs. Cut the log in half and use one half in this recipe and refrigerate the other half to crumble over a tossed green salad for another meal. The cheese will keep for 7 to 10 days in the refrigerator. If you have a nonstick 10-inch skillet with sloped sides (omelet pan) and are watching your fat and calorie intake, you may omit one or two egg yolks and reduce the amount of butter to 1 tablespoon for the potatoes and omit the tablespoon of butter for the omelet.

- 2 cups (8 ounces) frozen hash brown potatoes with peppers and onions (O'Brien style)
- 3 tablespoons butter or margarine, divided
- 4 large eggs
- 2 tablespoons milk or water
- ¼ teaspoon salt
- ⅛ teaspoon freshly ground black pepper
- 1 plum tomato
- 2 ounces goat cheese (chèvre) or herbed goat cheese
- 1 tablespoon chopped fresh chives or basil

Preheat oven to 200°F. Thaw potatoes in a microwave oven on HIGH for about 3 minutes. Meanwhile, melt 2 tablespoons butter in a 10-inch skillet with sloped sides. Add thawed potatoes and cook over medium-high heat for 5 minutes or until potatoes are browned, stirring occasionally.

While potatoes are cooking, beat eggs with milk, salt, and pepper and set aside. Transfer cooked potatoes to two dinner plates. Sprinkle with salt and pepper to taste, if desired. Place in oven to keep potatoes warm while preparing the omelet.

Add remaining 1 tablespoon butter to the same skillet. Swirl butter around the edges of skillet to prevent omelet from sticking. Add egg mixture and cook over medium heat for 2 minutes or until eggs begin to set on bottom. Gently lift edges of omelet with a spatula to allow uncooked portion of eggs to flow to edges and set. Continue cooking for 2 minutes or until center is almost set. While eggs are cooking, dice the tomato. Crumble cheese evenly over omelet, leaving a 1-inch-wide border. Sprinkle with tomato and chives. Using a large spatula, fold one edge over the filling. Cut omelet in half. Use pot holders to remove plates from oven. Transfer omelet halves to warm plates with potatoes.

🕑 *Serving suggestion:* Serve with crusty French bread.

2

Grilled, Broiled, and Roasted Meals

One-dish meals do not have to be limited to soups and stews. This chapter offers a variety of hearty meals that can be cooked up in a broiler pan, roasting pan, or grill rack.

A note about the grilled recipes: gas grills preheat quickly and will allow you to prepare the meals in the twenty-minute time frame, but if you are using a charcoal grill your overall preparation time will, of course, be longer as you must wait for the coals to reach cooking temperature.

Oven and broiler temperatures vary from gas to electric. The cooking times are a guide and may need to be slightly adjusted according to the desired doneness of the food. In the broiling recipes, the distance from the heat source is important to follow so as not to burn or undercook the food. Before preheating the broiler, place an empty broiler pan under the heating element and measure the distance from the heat source with a ruler to about ½ inch above the pan (where the food will eventually be). Adjust the rack to fit the range in inches the recipe calls for. Often, the oven racks are several inches apart and raising the rack one level is too much. If need be, you may use the lower rack and place an inverted jelly roll pan under the broiler pan to raise it another inch.

OVEN-FRIED FISH AND CHIPS

MAKES 2 SERVINGS

Don't worry if your oven hasn't reached 475°F by the time you are ready to put the fish and chips in . . . the fish will be sizzling and cooked through in just 9 minutes of baking time. For a Creole-style spicy flavor, use the blackened seasoning mix and hot pepper sauce.

3 cups (12 ounces) frozen seasoned french-fried
    potatoes
Nonstick vegetable spray
¼ cup seasoned dry bread crumbs
¼ teaspoon salt
⅛ teaspoon freshly ground black pepper
1 egg
1 tablespoon milk or water
1 tablespoon all-purpose flour
½ teaspoon Cajun, Creole, or blackened
    seasoning mix (optional)
2 4- to 5-ounce Boston scrod, orange roughy, or
    skinless catfish fillets, not more than ½ inch
    thick
1 tablespoon butter or margarine

TARTAR SAUCE:

¼ cup light mayonnaise
2 tablespoons pickle relish
1 teaspoon Dijon or yellow mustard
¼ teaspoon hot pepper sauce (optional)
Lemon wedges for garnish

Preheat oven to 475°F. Thaw potatoes in a microwave oven on HIGH for about 3 minutes. Coat a 15″ × 10″ jelly roll pan with nonstick vegetable cooking spray. Combine bread crumbs, salt, and pepper in a

24

shallow plate. Beat together egg and milk in another shallow plate. Place flour and, if desired, seasoning mix in a plastic bag. Add fish; shake bag to coat lightly with flour. Dip each fish fillet in egg mixture, turning to coat. Let excess egg mixture drip off. Dip fish into bread crumb mixture, turning to coat lightly. Place fish on prepared jelly roll pan. Arrange potatoes around fish. Melt butter in microwave-safe custard cup or small bowl on HIGH for about 1 minute. Spoon butter evenly over fish. Bake for 8 to 9 minutes or until fish is opaque and potatoes are hot.

Meanwhile, for tartar sauce, combine mayonnaise, pickle relish, mustard, and, if desired, hot pepper sauce. Serve fish and potatoes with sauce and lemon wedges.

Serving suggestion: Serve with chilled deli coleslaw.

Pescado Casserole Vera Cruz

MAKES 4 SERVINGS

Try this delicious south-of-the-border fish dinner on busy working week-nights. Picante sauce works better than salsa in this recipe because there is more liquid to cover the fish and beans.

> Nonstick vegetable spray
> 4 5- to 6-ounce fish fillets such as orange roughy
>   or talapia, not more than ½ inch thick
> 1 tablespoon fresh lime juice
> 1 16-ounce can pinto beans, drained
> 2 medium zucchini or yellow squash (or one of
>   each)
> ¾ cup prepared picante sauce, divided
> ¾ teaspoon ground cumin
> 1 cup (4 ounces) shredded cojack or cheddar
>   cheese
> Chopped cilantro (optional)

Preheat broiler. Coat the bottom of a broiler pan or shallow roasting pan with vegetable spray. Arrange fish in one layer in the center of the pan. Drizzle with lime juice. Broil 6 to 7 inches from heat source for 6 minutes.

Meanwhile, place beans in a medium bowl. Coarsely chop zucchini and add to bowl. Add ½ cup picante sauce and cumin; mix well. Remove pan from broiler. Spoon remaining ¼ cup picante sauce over fish. Arrange bean mixture around fish. Return pan to broiler and broil for 8 to 9 minutes or until fish is opaque and bean mixture is hot. Sprinkle cheese evenly over fish and bean mixture. Return to broiler for 1 minute to melt cheese. Sprinkle with cilantro, if desired.

🕐 *Serving suggestion:* Serve with warm corn tortillas or wedges of melon.

ROASTED SALMON DINNER

MAKES 4 SERVINGS

The oven temperature does not have to reach 450°F before you put in the pan of salmon and asparagus.

Nonstick vegetable spray
4 6-ounce salmon fillets, not more than ¾ inch
    thick
1 bunch (about 1 pound) asparagus spears
¼ cup light or regular bottled Caesar salad
    dressing
4 crusty herb or Italian rolls
Grated Parmesan cheese (optional)

Preheat oven to 450°F. Coat a shallow roasting pan or 15″ × 10″ jelly roll pan with nonstick vegetable spray. Place salmon skin-side down in pan. Rinse asparagus and break off tough stems; add to pan. Brush salmon and asparagus evenly with dressing. Place pan in oven and roast for 14 minutes or until salmon is opaque and asparagus is crisp-tender. Add rolls to pan or set directly on oven rack during the last 3 to 4 minutes of roasting time to heat through. Sprinkle asparagus with cheese, if desired.

🕐 *Serving suggestion:* Serve with a chilled deli new-potato salad.

BROILED CHICKEN PARMESAN

MAKES 2 SERVINGS

Using a foil-lined jelly roll pan or cookie sheet makes for easy cleanup after this quick chicken supper.

> 6 ounces (about 2 cups) frozen cottage fry
> potatoes
> ¼ cup seasoned dry bread crumbs
> ¼ cup grated Parmesan cheese
> ⅛ teaspoon cayenne pepper
> 1 egg
> 1 tablespoon water
> 2 skinless, boneless chicken breast halves
> 1 large zucchini or yellow squash, cut into ½-
> inch-thick slices
> 2 tablespoons butter or margarine, melted
> Salt (optional)

Preheat broiler. Thaw potatoes in a microwave oven on HIGH for about 2 minutes.

Meanwhile, combine bread crumbs, cheese, and cayenne pepper in a shallow dish or pie plate. Beat together egg and water in another shallow dish or pie plate. Dip chicken and zucchini into egg mixture, then dip into crumb mixture, turning to coat. Transfer to a foil-lined jelly roll pan or cookie sheet. Arrange potatoes around outer edges of pan. Brush butter lightly over chicken, zucchini, and potatoes. Broil 5 inches from heat source for 5 minutes. Turn and broil for 5 minutes more or until chicken is cooked through and vegetables and potatoes are browned. Sprinkle potatoes with salt to taste, if desired.

Serving suggestion: Serve with slices of honeydew melon or cantaloupe.

GRILLED STEAK AND POTATO DINNER

In the late summer when fresh corn is at its peak, substitute 4 small ears of shucked corn on the cob for the bell peppers. There will be room on the grill to toast sliced bread to complete the meal. If you are preparing this dish using the broiler, wrap dinner rolls in foil and place on rack under the broiler to heat through.

> 12 large frozen potato wedges or spicy flavored
>   potato wedges
> 2 bell peppers, preferably one red and one yellow
> 4 beef tenderloin steaks, cut 1 inch thick*
> ¼ cup light or regular Caesar or Italian salad
>   dressing
> Sour cream (optional)

Prepare gas or charcoal grill or preheat broiler. Thaw potato wedges in a microwave oven on HIGH for about 3 minutes. Cut bell peppers lengthwise into quarters; discard stems and seeds. Brush both sides of steaks and peppers with dressing.

Place steaks, potatoes, and bell peppers on grill over medium-hot coals or on rack of broiler pan. Grill or broil 4 to 5 inches from heat source for 6 minutes. Turn steaks, potatoes, and bell peppers; continue grilling or broiling for about 5 minutes more for medium-rare steaks or until desired doneness. If desired, spoon sour cream over potatoes.

🕐 *Serving suggestion:* Serve with grilled bread or warm rolls.

Two well-trimmed beef top loin steaks, cut 1 inch thick, may be substituted. Cut each steak crosswise in half to form four steaks.

TUSCAN GRILLED LAMB DINNER

If garlic-flavored olive oil is not available, add 1 teaspoon bottled minced garlic to 3 tablespoons olive oil. The cooking times indicated below will result in lamb chops cooked to medium doneness.

> 3 tablespoons garlic-flavored olive oil
> 1 tablespoon balsamic vinegar
> ¼ teaspoon salt
> ¼ teaspoon freshly ground black pepper
> ½ teaspoon dried rosemary, crushed
> 4 6-ounce well-trimmed loin lamb chops, cut
>   1 inch thick
> 2 large tomatoes
> 4 small zucchini or yellow squash, halved
>   lengthwise
> 4 ½-inch-thick slices sourdough bread
> 2 to 3 tablespoons grated Parmesan or Asiago
>   cheese

Prepare grill or heat broiler. Combine oil, vinegar, salt, and pepper, mixing with a fork until well blended. Press rosemary into both sides of lamb chops. Cut tomatoes in half; push out seeds with finger. Brush cut sides of tomatoes, both sides of squash halves, and bread lightly with oil mixture. Brush remaining oil mixture on both sides of lamb chops.

For grill: place lamb chops and squash in center of grill over medium-high coals. Grill, covered, for 5 minutes. Turn lamb chops and squash; place tomatoes, cut-side up on grill. Cover grill; cook for 4 minutes. Transfer lamb chops and vegetables to serving plates. Place bread on grill; grill for 1 to 2 minutes per side or until lightly toasted. Sprinkle tomatoes and squash with cheese.

For broiler: place lamb chops and squash on rack of broiler pan.

Broil 4 to 5 inches from heat source for 5 minutes. Turn lamb chops and squash; place tomatoes, cut-side up on rack of broiler pan. Broil for 4 minutes. Transfer lamb chops and vegetables to serving plates. Place bread on rack of broiler pan; broil for 30 seconds per side or until lightly toasted. Sprinkle tomatoes and squash with cheese.

☺ *Serving suggestion:* Serve with a salad of mixed bitter greens tossed with vinaigrette dressing.

PAPRIKASH PORK CHOPS WITH WARM GARLIC BREAD

MAKES 4 SERVINGS

Sauerkraut in refrigerated jars has a crisper texture than canned sauerkraut. The leftover kraut keeps up to 8 weeks in the refrigerator. Look for bottled minced roasted garlic next to the minced garlic in the produce section of your supermarket.

> 4 6- to 8-ounce well-trimmed center-cut pork
>   chops, cut ½ to ¾ inch thick
> 2 teaspoons paprika, preferably Hungarian sweet,
>   plus additional for garnish
> ½ teaspoon salt
> ¼ teaspoon cayenne pepper or Hungarian hot
>   paprika
> ½ cup light or regular sour cream
> ½ cup well-drained sauerkraut
> 1 French bread baguette, about 12 inches long
> 2 tablespoons butter or margarine
> ½ teaspoon bottled minced garlic or roasted
>   garlic

Preheat broiler. Sprinkle chops on both sides with paprika, salt, and cayenne pepper and place on rack of broiler pan. Broil 4 to 5 inches from heat source for 4 minutes. Turn and continue broiling for 4 more minutes.

Meanwhile, combine sour cream and sauerkraut, mixing well. Cut bread in half lengthwise, then crosswise into quarters. Soften butter in microwave oven for about 15 seconds on HIGH. Combine softened butter and garlic and spread evenly over cut sides of bread.

Remove pan from broiler. Spoon sour cream mixture evenly over chops. Place bread, cut-side up alongside chops. Sprinkle chops and bread with additional paprika, if desired. Return to broiler; broil for 3 to 4 minutes or until chops are no longer pink in the center and bread is golden brown.

Serving suggestion: Serve with a spinach salad.

GRILLED VEAL CHOPS WITH PORTABELLO MUSHROOMS AND FRESH CORN

MAKES 4 SERVINGS

Veal chops can be expensive but are often on sale and worth the splurge. You may, however, prepare this easy grilled supper with pork chops and cook them until just barely pink in the center.

> 1 French bread baguette, about 12 inches long
> 2 tablespoons garlic infused olive oil *or*
>> 2 tablespoons olive oil plus ½ teaspoon bottled minced garlic
>
> 4 medium portabello mushrooms
> 4 ears fresh corn, shucked, or thawed frozen corn on the cob
> 4 6- to 8-ounce well-trimmed veal loin or rib chops, cut ¾ inch thick
> Salt
> Freshly ground black pepper
> ¾ teaspoon dried thyme leaves or crushed dried rosemary or a combination

Prepare gas or charcoal grill. Cut bread in half lengthwise, then crosswise into quarters. Brush oil lightly over cut sides of bread, mushrooms, corn, and chops; sprinkle lightly with salt and pepper, then with the herbs.

Place chops on center of grill over medium-hot coals. Arrange mushrooms and corn around chops. Grill, covered, for 5 minutes. Turn chops, mushrooms, and corn. Arrange bread cut-side down around edges of grill. Continue grilling, covered, for 5 to 6 minutes or until chops are desired doneness and vegetables are tender. Remove bread when lightly toasted.

🕐 *Serving suggestion:* Serve with a Caesar salad.

3

Soups, Stews, and
Potato Toppers

Do we ever tire of a comforting bowl of soup or a steaming stew? Can we really go a whole week without eating a baked potato? These perfect one-dish meals contain protein and vegetables and either a starch, grain, or pasta. And every recipe in this chapter gives you a variety of each.

BOUILLABAISSE

MAKES 4 SERVINGS

For this quick version of the quintessential fish stew, purchase home-made-type garlic croutons from your local bakery or supermarket. If frozen, raw, peeled and deveined shrimp are not available, purchase cooked cleaned shrimp and add them during the last few minutes of cooking to heat through.

- 1 tablespoon olive oil
- 1 teaspoon bottled minced garlic
- 1 14½-ounce can pasta-ready, seasoned diced tomatoes or Italian-style stewed tomatoes, undrained
- 1 8-ounce bottle clam juice *or* 1 cup canned chicken broth
- ½ cup water
- ½ cup ditalini or small shell pasta
- ½ teaspoon dried thyme leaves
- ½ teaspoon saffron threads, crushed *or* ¼ teaspoon ground saffron *or* ½ teaspoon turmeric
- ¼ to ½ teaspoon hot pepper sauce, as desired
- ½ pound skinless sea bass, halibut, or red snapper fish fillets
- ½ pound frozen or fresh peeled and deveined medium shrimp
- 2 tablespoons chopped fresh basil (optional)
- 1 cup garlic croutons

Heat oil in a large, deep skillet or dutch oven over medium-high heat. Add garlic and sauté for 1 minute. Add tomatoes, clam juice, water, pasta, thyme, saffron, and pepper sauce. Cover and bring to a boil over high heat. Stir well and reduce heat to medium. Cover and continue simmering for 5 minutes.

Meanwhile, cut the fish into 1-inch pieces. Stir fish and shrimp into the tomato mixture. Cover and simmer for 5 minutes over medium-high heat or until pasta is tender and fish and shrimp are opaque. Ladle into shallow bowls and sprinkle with basil, if desired. Garnish with croutons.

🕐 *Serving suggestion*: Serve with a Caesar salad.

Easy Clam Chowder

MAKES 4 SERVINGS

A true New England clam chowder relies on salt pork for its unique flavor, but smoked bacon gives this speedy version just as much taste.

> 2 cups (8 ounces) frozen hash brown potatoes
>   with peppers and onions (O'Brien style)
> 2 thick slices or 3 regular slices bacon, preferably
>   apple wood smoked
> 2 tablespoons all-purpose flour
> 2 cups milk
> ¼ teaspoon salt, or to taste
> ¼ teaspoon freshly ground black pepper
> 2 6½-ounce cans minced clams, undrained
> Oyster crackers

Thaw potatoes in microwave oven on HIGH for about 2 minutes. Cut bacon into ¼-inch pieces and cook in a large saucepan over medium-high heat for 2 minutes. Add the flour and cook for 1 minute, stirring frequently. Stir in milk, salt, and pepper; cook for 1 minute, stirring constantly. Stir in potatoes and simmer, uncovered, over medium-low heat for 5 minutes, stirring occasionally. (Mixture will be very thick.) Stir in clams and their liquid; heat through, 3 to 4 minutes, stirring occasionally. Serve with oyster crackers and additional freshly ground black pepper.

Serving suggestion: Serve with a marinated vegetable salad or coleslaw.

TURKEY TORTILLA SOUP

MAKES 4 SERVINGS

Tortilla chips give this delicious soup its thickness and delightful corn flavor.

> 2 14½-ounce cans reduced sodium chicken broth
> 2 cups (4 ounces) broken lightly salted tortilla
>   chips
> 8 ounces smoked or regular deli turkey breast,
>   cut ½ inch thick
> ½ cup prepared picante sauce, preferably
>   medium hot
> 1 teaspoon ground cumin
> ½ cup (2 ounces) shredded Monterey Jack or
>   cheddar cheese
> ¼ cup chopped cilantro or thinly sliced scallions
>   (optional)

Bring broth to a boil in a covered medium saucepan over high heat. Stir in tortilla chips and remove from heat. Let stand, covered, for 6 minutes. Meanwhile, cut the turkey into ½-inch pieces and set aside.

Puree the tortilla mixture in batches in a food processor or blender; return to saucepan. Add turkey, picante sauce, and cumin and mix well. Cook over medium-high heat until heated through, about 2 minutes, stirring occasionally. Ladle into soup bowls and top with cheese. Sprinkle with cilantro or scallions, if desired.

Serving suggestion: Serve with a tossed green salad.

MILANESE GNOCCHI EN BRODO

MAKES 4 SERVINGS

Gnocchi are Italian dumplings made from potatoes. Occasionally you will find fresh gnocchi in markets that sell fresh pasta, but frozen and shelf stable gnocchi are available in many supermarkets.

This recipe is perfect for using any leftover cooked or rotisserie chicken, but you may also use deli turkey breast. Purchase a ½-inch slice and dice the meat while the broth comes to a boil. Purchase bags of washed spinach in the produce department or from the salad bar of your supermarket. If fresh basil is not available, add 2 teaspoons dried basil to the skillet along with the chicken.

2 14½-ounce cans chicken or vegetable broth
¼ teaspoon dried hot red pepper flakes
8 ounces frozen or shelf stable gnocchi (potato
   dumplings)
2 teaspoons bottled minced garlic
1½ cups coarsely chopped or shredded cooked
   chicken
2 plum tomatoes *or* 1 large tomato, coarsely
   chopped
2 cups packed torn spinach leaves, stems
   removed
2 tablespoons sliced fresh basil leaves
½ cup freshly grated Parmesan, Romano, or
   Asiago cheese

Combine broth and pepper flakes in a large deep skillet. Cover and bring to a boil over high heat. Uncover and add the gnocchi and garlic; return to a boil. Reduce heat to medium and simmer, uncovered, for 3 to 4 minutes or until the gnocchi begin to float to the top of liquid. Stir in the chicken and simmer for 2 minutes. Add tomatoes and spinach leaves and cook for 1 to 2 minutes or until spinach wilts. Ladle into shallow bowls and top with basil and cheese.

Serving suggestion: Serve with garlic or sesame bread sticks.

BARLEY, BEEF, AND MUSHROOM CHOWDER

MAKES 3 TO 4 SERVINGS:

To avoid toughening the meat, be sure to purchase rare roast beef from the deli and stir into soup just to heat through. You may substitute left-over cooked steak or home cooked roast beef, if desired. This is a fairly thick soup. If a thinner version is desired, add additional broth or milk or reduce the flour to 1½ teaspoons. For a meatless version, replace the beef broth with vegetable broth and omit the roast beef.

2 tablespoons butter or margarine
1 cup chopped onion (frozen or fresh)
2 cups (8 ounces) sliced fresh mushrooms
1 14½-ounce can beef broth
⅓ cup quick-cooking pearl barley
½ teaspoon dried thyme leaves
¼ teaspoon salt
¼ teaspoon freshly ground black pepper
1 cup milk
1 tablespoon all-purpose flour
6 ounces rare deli roast beef, cut ¼ inch thick
1 tablespoon dry sherry (optional)

Melt butter in a large saucepan over medium-high heat. Add the onion and mushrooms and cook for 2 minutes, stirring occasionally. Stir in broth, barley, thyme, salt, and pepper and bring to a boil over high heat. Simmer, uncovered for 10 minutes.

Meanwhile, combine the milk and flour, mixing well. Cut roast beef into ¼-inch dice. Stir the milk mixture into the soup and simmer for 3 minutes or until barley is tender and soup thickens, stirring frequently. Stir in roast beef and heat through. Stir in sherry, if desired.

Serving suggestion: Serve with pumpernickel bread.

Hearty Ham and Navy Bean Soup

MAKES 4 TO 5 SERVINGS

For a thicker soup, partially mash 1 can of the beans in a bowl with a potato masher or the back of a wooden spoon.

> 1 tablespoon vegetable oil
> 1 cup chopped onion (frozen or fresh)
> 1 teaspoon bottled minced garlic
> 2 16-ounce cans navy or great northern beans, drained
> 1 14½-ounce can vegetable or chicken broth
> 1 14½-ounce can diced tomatoes in juice, undrained
> 8 ounces fully cooked smoked ham slice, cut about ½ inch thick
> ½ teaspoon dried sage
> ¼ teaspoon freshly ground black pepper
> 2 tablespoons chopped fresh parsley (optional)

Heat oil in a large saucepan over medium heat. Add the onion and garlic and cook for 5 minutes, stirring occasionally. Add beans, broth, and tomatoes. Cover and bring to a boil over high heat.

Meanwhile, cut the ham into ½-inch cubes. Stir ham, sage, and pepper into soup. Cover, reduce heat, and simmer for 6 minutes. Stir in parsley, if desired.

🕐 *Serving suggestion:* Serve with corn bread or corn muffins.

MIDWESTERN SALMON STEW

MAKES 4 SERVINGS

Door County, Wisconsin, is famous for outdoor fish boils where a cauldron of the freshest fish and vegetables cooks over an open flame to feed a crowd of hungry onlookers. This version is just as tasty, but cooks in only twenty minutes. In Wisconsin, lake trout or whitefish steaks are typically used, but they are harder to find fresh in other parts of the country. Salmon has a wonderful texture when poached in this manner. You may use any variety of salmon such as coho, sockeye, Alaskan, or Norwegian. The peppercorns will flavor the broth, but should be left in the pan when the stew is ladled out.

1 14½-ounce can vegetable broth
8 ounces baby carrots
½ cup water
2 teaspoons whole black peppercorns
1 pound red potatoes
1 cup coarsely chopped sweet or yellow onion
4 salmon or lake trout steaks, cut ½ inch thick
   (about 1¼ pounds)
¼ teaspoon salt

OPTIONAL TOPPINGS FOR FISH:

2 tablespoons melted butter
¼ cup light or regular sour cream plus
   1 teaspoon horseradish

Combine broth, carrots, water, and peppercorns in a large deep skillet. Cover and bring to a boil over high heat. Meanwhile, scrub the potatoes and cut into 1-inch pieces. Stir potatoes and onion into broth mixture, cover, and return to a boil. Reduce heat to medium-low and simmer, covered, for 10 minutes.

Arrange salmon steaks over vegetables and sprinkle with salt. Cover and simmer for 5 minutes or until salmon is opaque. Ladle into shallow soup bowls. If desired, drizzle fish with butter or serve with horseradish cream.

Serving suggestion: Serve with sourdough bread.

RED LENTIL AND CHICKEN STEW

MAKES 4 SERVINGS

Look for red or orange lentils by the dried beans. They cook much more quickly than green or brown lentils and add a beautiful color and interesting flavor to this hearty stew. For a spicy stew, add ¼ teaspoon Hungarian hot paprika or cayenne pepper.

2 14½-ounce cans vegetable or chicken broth
¾ cup red lentils
1 16-ounce package frozen stew vegetables
     (potatoes, carrots, onions, and celery or
     potatoes, peas, and carrots)
1½ cups diced cooked chicken, turkey, or fully
     cooked ham or sausage
1 teaspoon dried thyme leaves
1 teaspoon paprika
¼ teaspoon freshly ground black pepper

Combine broth and lentils in a large saucepan. Cover and bring to a boil over high heat. Reduce heat and simmer, covered, for 10 minutes. Meanwhile, thaw the vegetables in a microwave oven on HIGH for about 3 minutes or in a colander under warm running water.

Stir the vegetables, chicken, thyme, paprika, and pepper into the broth mixture. Increase heat to high. Cover and simmer for 3 minutes or until lentils are tender.

Serving suggestion: Serve with warm pita bread or pita chips.

SICILIAN RAVIOLI STEW

MAKES 4 SERVINGS

Calamata olives are used frequently in Sicilian cuisine. If olives are unpitted, whack them with the side of a chef's knife or a meat mallet so that the olives split and the pit is exposed.

> 1 9-ounce package cheese- or meat-filled
>   refrigerated fresh ravioli
> 1 14½-ounce can vegetable or chicken broth
> ¾ cup water or additional broth
> ⅛ teaspoon dried hot red pepper flakes (optional)
> 1 medium yellow squash
> 1 medium zucchini squash
> 2 cloves garlic, minced, *or* 1 teaspoon bottled
>   minced garlic
> 1 8-ounce can stewed tomatoes, undrained
> 1 teaspoon dried basil
> 1 teaspoon dried oregano or marjoram
> ⅓ cup calamata olives, pitted and coarsely
>   chopped
> ½ cup (2 ounces) freshly grated Parmesan or
>   Romano cheese

Place a large deep skillet over high heat. Add ravioli, broth, water, and, if desired, pepper flakes. Cover and bring to a boil. Reduce heat and simmer, covered, for 5 minutes.

Meanwhile, cut the yellow squash and zucchini crosswise into ½-inch slices; cut each slice into quarters. Add squash, garlic, tomatoes, basil, and oregano to skillet. Cover and continue to simmer for 7 to 8 minutes or until ravioli and vegetables are tender. Stir in olives and ladle into shallow bowls. Top with cheese.

☺ *Serving suggestion:* Serve with garlic bread.

HEARTY BEEF STEW

MAKES 4 SERVINGS

Tenderloin tips are the end pieces of the most tender cut of beef, the tenderloin muscle. They are usually much lower in price than tenderloin steaks or roasts and work well in this quick weeknight stew. When whole tenderloins are on sale, purchase one for several meals. Cut the center section into a roast or steaks and freeze. Use the tips for this recipe.

> 1 tablespoon garlic infused olive oil *or*
>   1 tablespoon olive oil plus 1 teaspoon bottled
>   minced garlic
> 1 pound beef tenderloin tips, cut into 1-inch
>   pieces
> ½ teaspoon salt
> ¼ teaspoon freshly ground black pepper
> 1 16-ounce package frozen stew vegetables
>   (potatoes, carrots, onions, and celery or
>   potatoes, peas, and carrots)
> 2½ cups canned beef broth, divided
> 1 teaspoon dried thyme leaves
> 2 tablespoons cornstarch

Heat oil in a large deep skillet over medium-high heat. Add meat, salt, and pepper and stir-fry for 3 minutes or until meat is no longer pink. Transfer the mixture to a bowl and set aside.

Meanwhile, thaw the vegetables in a microwave oven on HIGH for about 3 minutes or in a colander under warm running water. Add 2¼ cups broth, thyme, and thawed vegetables to the same skillet. Cover and bring to a boil over high heat. Reduce heat, cover, and simmer for 5 minutes or until vegetables are tender. Combine remaining ¼ cup broth and cornstarch, mixing until smooth. Stir into stew. Cook, uncovered, for 2 minutes or until thickened, stirring occasionally. Stir in reserved meat with any accumulated juices and heat through. Ladle into shallow bowls.

🕐 *Serving suggestion:* Serve with crusty rye rolls.

TORTELLINI VEGETABLE STEW

MAKES 4 SERVINGS

Look for a variety of flavored fresh tortellini in the refrigerated section of your supermarket. If you do not find packaged, washed, and cut assorted vegetables in the produce section of your supermarket, purchase a mixture of your favorite cut vegetables from the salad bar.

> 2 14½-ounce cans chicken or vegetable broth
> 1 9-ounce package refrigerated fresh tortellini
> 2 cups (about 8 ounces) assorted, fresh, cut, mixed vegetables
> 1 teaspoon bottled minced garlic
> ½ cup (2 ounces) freshly grated Parmesan or Asiago cheese
> Rosemary, basil, or black pepper infused olive oil (optional)

Place a large deep skillet over high heat. Add broth, tortellini, vegetables, and garlic. Cover and bring to a boil. Reduce heat and simmer, covered, for about 12 minutes or until tortellini and vegetables are tender, stirring once. Transfer to shallow soup bowls and sprinkle with cheese. Drizzle lightly with infused oil, if desired.

Serving suggestion: Serve with crusty Italian rolls.

ITALIAN-STYLE WHITE BEAN AND SAUSAGE CHILI

MAKES 4 SERVINGS

Try Italy's version of chili for a hearty weeknight supper. Look for a variety of fully cooked sausages in your grocer's meat case or substitute Polish sausage for the Italian sausage. If fresh fennel is not available substitute 1 cup of chopped onion.

1 tablespoon olive oil
1 small fennel bulb
2 teaspoons bottled minced garlic
8 ounces fully cooked Italian sausage
½ cup canned beef or chicken broth
1 8-ounce can stewed tomatoes, undrained
1 teaspoon dried rosemary, crushed
1 16- to 19-ounce can cannellini beans, drained
Freshly ground black pepper
Garlic croutons (optional)

Heat oil in a large saucepan over medium heat. Chop enough fennel bulb to measure 1 cup. Cook the fennel and garlic in oil for 5 minutes, stirring once. If desired, chop feathery fennel fronds and set aside for garnish.

Meanwhile, cut the sausage crosswise into ¼-inch slices. Add sausage, broth, tomatoes, and rosemary to skillet, cover, and simmer for 5 minutes. Stir in beans, cover, and continue to cook for 4 minutes or until fennel is tender. Ladle into shallow bowls and top with reserved fennel fronds, if desired. Sprinkle with pepper to taste. Top with croutons, if desired.

Serving suggestion: Serve with a tossed green salad.

Cajun Shrimp–Topped Potatoes

MAKES 2 SERVINGS

If frozen, raw, peeled and deveined shrimp are not available, call ahead before your trip to the supermarket and ask the seafood department if they will peel and devein raw shrimp for you and omit the thawing step. Since the shrimp mixture cooks so quickly there is time to peel and mince fresh garlic for this meal, but you may look for containers of refrigerated peeled garlic cloves in your supermarket produce section to eliminate the peeling step. This garlic is more costly than heads of fresh garlic, but the cloves are ready to put through a garlic press. The peeled garlic cloves will keep in the refrigerator for up to 3 weeks.

> 4 medium baking potatoes
> 1 pound frozen, raw, peeled and deveined
>   medium or large shrimp
> 1 16-ounce package frozen bell pepper and onion
>   strips for stir-fry
> 2 tablespoons butter or margarine
> 4 garlic cloves, minced
> 1 teaspoon Cajun, Creole, or blackened
>   seasoning mix
> ¾ cup canned vegetable broth
> 1 tablespoon cornstarch
> Salt (optional)
> Chopped fresh parsley or fresh thyme leaves
>   (optional)

Scrub potatoes and prick them in several places with the tip of a sharp knife. Place potatoes on a paper towel in a microwave oven and cook on HIGH for 7 minutes. Turn potatoes over and continue to cook on HIGH for 8 to 9 minutes or until tender.

Meanwhile, place the shrimp and vegetable strips in a colander. Thaw under warm running water for about 3 minutes and drain well.

Melt butter in large skillet over medium-high heat. Add garlic and drained shrimp and vegetables; sprinkle with seasoning mix. Cook for 3 to 4 minutes or until shrimp are opaque, stirring frequently. Combine broth and cornstarch, mixing until smooth. Stir into shrimp mixture and cook for 1 to 2 minutes or until sauce has thickened, stirring occasionally.

Split hot potatoes with a fork and squeeze the ends inward to fluff. If desired, sprinkle lightly with salt to taste. Spoon shrimp mixture over the potatoes. Sprinkle with parsley, if desired.

🕐 *Serving suggestion:* Serve with a Caesar salad.

CHICKEN AND
MUSHROOM–TOPPED POTATOES

MAKES 4 SERVINGS

Look for small packages of dried porcini mushrooms in your super-market produce section where you will also find plastic bags of peeled baby carrots. The dried mushrooms give the sauce an earthy, robust flavor usually found only in slowly cooked sauces.

> 4 medium baking potatoes
> 1 14½-ounce can chicken broth
> ½ cup water
> 2 cups (8 ounces) baby carrots
> 2 cups (8 ounces) frozen pearl onions
> ½ ounce dried porcini mushrooms
> 1 teaspoon dried thyme leaves
> ¼ teaspoon salt
> ¼ teaspoon freshly ground black pepper
> 1 pound chicken tenders or boneless, skinless
>   chicken breast
> 1½ tablespoons butter or margarine
> 2 tablespoons all-purpose flour

Scrub potatoes and prick them in several places with the tip of a sharp knife. Place potatoes on a paper towel in a microwave oven and cook on HIGH for 7 minutes. Turn potatoes over and continue to cook on HIGH for 8 to 9 minutes or until tender.

Meanwhile, combine the broth, water, carrots, onions, and dried mushrooms in a large deep skillet. Cover and bring to a boil over high heat. Add thyme, salt, and pepper to broth mixture and simmer, uncovered, for 5 minutes.

Meanwhile, cut the chicken into 1-inch pieces and stir into the broth mixture. Simmer, uncovered, for 4 minutes. Place butter in a small custard cup or microwave-safe bowl and cook on HIGH for 10 to 15 seconds or until softened. Add flour and mix well. Stir flour mixture into stew. Simmer, uncovered, for 3 minutes or until sauce thickens and chicken is cooked through, stirring occasionally.

Split hot potatoes with a fork and squeeze the ends inward to fluff. If desired, sprinkle lightly with salt and pepper to taste. Spoon chicken mixture over the potatoes.

Serving suggestion: Serve with crusty whole-wheat rolls.

CURRIED CHICKEN AND VEGETABLE–TOPPED POTATOES

MAKES 4 SERVINGS

Enjoy traditional Indian flavors in this easy curry dish.

    4 medium baking potatoes
    1 16-ounce package frozen mixed vegetable
        medley such as broccoli, cauliflower, pearl
        onions, and red bell peppers
    1 tablespoon olive or vegetable oil
    12 ounces chicken or turkey breast cut for stir-fry
    2 teaspoons bottled minced garlic
    2 teaspoons curry powder
    ⅛ teaspoon cayenne pepper
    2 tablespoons all-purpose flour
    1¼ cups canned chicken or vegetable broth
    ⅓ cup thinly sliced scallions
    Salt and pepper (optional)
    Chopped peanuts (optional)
    Shredded coconut (optional)

Scrub potatoes and prick them in several places with the tip of a sharp knife. Place potatoes on a paper towel in a microwave oven and cook on HIGH for 7 minutes. Turn potatoes over and continue to cook on HIGH for 8 to 9 minutes or until tender.

Meanwhile, thaw the vegetables in a colander under warm running water. Heat oil in a large deep skillet over medium-high heat. Add the chicken and garlic. Sprinkle with curry powder and cayenne pepper and stir-fry for 3 minutes. Add the flour and stir-fry for 1 minute. Add broth and vegetables and simmer for 4 minutes or until sauce thickens, stirring frequently. Stir in the scallions.

Split hot potatoes with a fork and squeeze the ends inward to fluff. If desired, sprinkle lightly with salt and pepper to taste. Spoon chicken mixture over the potatoes. Top with chopped peanuts and shredded coconut, if desired.

⊕ *Serving suggestion:* Serve with bottled mango chutney.

BEEF STROGANOFF–TOPPED POTATOES

MAKES 4 SERVINGS

If sliced mushrooms are not available, purchase 8 ounces sliced mushrooms from the supermarket salad bar and omit the rinsing step.

- 4 medium baking potatoes
- 2 tablespoons butter or margarine
- 1 small onion, chopped
- 1 8-ounce package sliced mushrooms, rinsed, patted dry with paper towels
- 12 ounces beef tenderloin tips or steaks, cut into ¾-inch pieces
- ½ teaspoon salt
- ½ teaspoon Hungarian sweet paprika
- ¼ teaspoon freshly ground black pepper
- 1 cup canned beef broth
- ½ cup light or regular sour cream
- 1 tablespoon all-purpose flour
- Chopped fresh chives or parsley (optional)

Scrub potatoes and prick them in several places with the tip of a sharp knife. Place potatoes on a paper towel in a microwave oven and cook on HIGH for 7 minutes. Turn potatoes over and continue to cook on HIGH for 8 to 9 minutes or until tender.

Meanwhile, melt butter in a large skillet. Add onion and cook over medium-high heat for 2 minutes. Add mushrooms and cook for 3 minutes, stirring occasionally. Add beef and sprinkle with salt, paprika, and pepper. Cook for 5 minutes, stirring frequently. Add broth and bring to a boil. Combine sour cream and flour, mixing well. Stir into the beef mixture. Cook for 1 minute or until sauce thickens, stirring constantly.

Split hot potatoes with a fork and squeeze the ends inward to fluff. If desired, sprinkle lightly with salt and pepper to taste. Spoon beef mixture over the potatoes. Sprinkle with chives, if desired.

Serving suggestion: Serve with a spinach salad.

GUADALAJARA CHILI CON CARNE

The traditional version of this tasty recipe calls for slowly cooking pork shoulder, but thanks to quick-cooking pork tenderloin, supper is ready in no time! Reheat any leftovers and serve over hot baked potatoes or in flour tortillas with shredded cheddar cheese for quick burritos.

1 tablespoon vegetable oil
1 cup chopped onion (frozen or fresh)
2 teaspoons bottled minced garlic
1 12- to 14-ounce well-trimmed pork tenderloin
2 teaspoons chili powder
2 teaspoons ground cumin
2 16-ounce cans chili beans in spicy sauce,
    undrained
1 14½-ounce can Mexican-style or chili-style
    stewed tomatoes, undrained
½ cup salsa or picante sauce
½ cup coarsely chopped cilantro
½ cup light or regular sour cream
½ cup shredded cheddar cheese

Heat oil in a large deep skillet. Add onion and garlic and cook over medium-high heat for 2 minutes. Meanwhile, cut the pork into ¾-inch cubes, adding it to the skillet as it is cut. Sprinkle pork with chili powder and cumin and cook for 3 minutes, stirring occasionally.

Stir in beans, tomatoes, and salsa. Cover and bring to a boil. Reduce heat and simmer, covered, for 10 minutes. Stir cilantro into the chili and ladle into shallow bowls. Top with sour cream and cheese.

🕐 *Serving suggestion:* Serve with warm tortillas, corn muffins, or tortilla chips.

4

Pastas and Pizzas

Hardly a week goes by that families don't indulge in a pasta or pizza dinner. But a pasta dinner in only one pot? Yes! Thanks to quick cooking pastas such as orzo and cappellini and the refrigerated, fresh pastas that cook in just minutes, a wide variety of meals may be prepared in a single large saucepan, dutch oven, or pasta cooking pot. Adding vegetables to the water during the pasta cooking time saves time and eliminates the need to wash another pan. Remember, to bring a pot of water or other liquid to a boil quickly, cover it and place it over the highest heat. If you have an electric range, start the burner even before you fill up the pot!

Thanks to widely available prepared pizza crusts, the pizza recipes will only require an oven rack (not even a pizza pan to wash!). The crust on these quick-cooking pizzas will be golden brown and crisp even in the 8 or 9 minutes of baking time. It is very helpful to have a flat cookie sheet or very large spatula with which to retrieve the pizza. Make sure to preheat the oven at the onset of the pizza recipes, but don't worry if the correct temperature isn't reached by the time you are ready to bake the pizza. The pizza will still be hot and crusty with the cheese melted in just 10 minutes of baking time. If there are crumbs from the bottom of the pizza crust on your oven floor, you may easily wipe them out when the oven is completely cooled before you use it the next time.

Pan-Seared Sea Bass with Bok Choy and Oriental Noodles

MAKES 4 SERVINGS

Bok choy, a leafy vegetable with thick sweet stalks is usually available year-round, but you may substitute 3 cups sliced napa or Chinese cabbage. Look for Oriental sesame oil, hot chili oil, straw mushrooms, and curly Chinese noodles in the ethnic section of your supermarket.

> 1 tablespoon Oriental sesame oil
> 1 tablespoon all-purpose flour
> 1 teaspoon ground ginger
> 4 5-ounce skinless sea bass or orange roughy fish
>   fillets, no more than ½ inch thick
> 1 tablespoon soy sauce
> 2 14½-ounce cans Oriental broth or chicken
>   broth
> ½ teaspoon hot chili oil (optional)
> 1 5-ounce package curly Chinese noodles
> 1 small head bok choy
> 1 6-ounce can *or* 8-ounce jar straw mushrooms,
>   drained (optional)

Preheat oven to 200°F. Heat sesame oil in a large deep nonstick skillet over medium-high heat. Meanwhile, combine the flour and ginger on a plate. Dip fish into flour mixture, turning to coat lightly. Cook in hot oil for 3 minutes per side or until fish is opaque. Transfer fish to four dinner plates with raised rims. Drizzle soy sauce over fish and place plates in the oven to keep warm while preparing noodles.

Add broth and, if desired, chili oil to the same skillet. Add noodles, cover, and bring to a boil over high heat. Uncover and stir the noodles to separate them. Reduce heat, cover, and continue to simmer for 3 minutes. Meanwhile, cut bok choy crosswise through stems and leaves into ¼-inch slices. Stir into noodle mixture and increase heat to high. Stir in mushrooms, if desired. Cook, uncovered, for about 2 minutes or until noodles are tender (bok choy will be crisp-tender). Using a pot holder, remove plates from oven. Spoon noodle mixture alongside fish. Serve with additional soy sauce, if desired.

Serving suggestion: Serve with fresh pineapple wedges.

ANGEL HAIR PASTA WITH CLAM SAUCE

MAKES 4 SERVINGS

For this dish, fresh garlic is a must! Look for plastic jars of peeled garlic cloves in the refrigerated produce section of your supermarket. The garlic keeps up to 3 weeks in the refrigerator.

The chopped clams are stirred in at the end of the cooking time so they do not toughen.

> 2 tablespoons olive oil
> 3 cloves peeled garlic forced through a garlic press or minced
> 3 6½-ounce cans chopped clams
> ⅛ teaspoon dried hot red pepper flakes
> 1 14½-ounce can pasta-ready diced tomatoes, undrained
> ¾ cup water
> 1 9-ounce package refrigerated fresh angel hair pasta
> 1 cup (4 ounces) freshly grated Parmesan cheese, divided
> Freshly ground black pepper (optional)

Heat oil in a large deep skillet over medium heat. Add garlic and cook for 1 minute, stirring occasionally. Open the cans of clams and drain the liquid into the skillet, reserving clams in can. Add pepper flakes to liquid and bring to a boil over high heat. Add tomatoes and water and boil gently for 4 minutes.

Add pasta, separating with two forks. Cover, reduce heat, and simmer for 3 minutes. Add reserved clams and ½ cup of cheese, tossing well. Transfer to dinner plates and sprinkle with remaining ½ cup of cheese. Serve with pepper, if desired.

⏱ *Serving suggestion:* Serve with garlic bread.

Mussels and Linguini Provençal-Style

MAKES 3 TO 4 SERVINGS

Look for prepared pesto in jars in the specialty foods section or in plastic tubs in the refrigerated pasta sauce section of your supermarket. You may substitute water for the dry white wine or vermouth if you prefer.

1 14½-ounce can chicken broth
1 14½-ounce can pasta-ready, seasoned diced
   tomatoes or diced tomatoes in juice, undrained
¼ cup dry white wine or vermouth
1 teaspoon bottled minced garlic
1 pound mussels
¼ cup prepared pesto
1 9-ounce package refrigerated fresh linguini
   pasta
Freshly grated Parmesan or Asiago cheese
   (optional)

Combine broth, tomatoes, wine, and garlic in a large deep skillet or dutch oven. Cover and bring to a boil over high heat. While the mixture comes to a boil, scrub mussels under cold running water and remove beards.

Add cleaned mussels to the skillet, cover, and cook over medium heat for 5 minutes or until mussels begin to open. Uncover and stir in pesto. Stir in linguini, separating with two forks. Simmer, uncovered, for 5 to 6 minutes or until pasta is tender and mussels are opened, stirring occasionally. Discard any mussels that have not opened. Ladle into shallow bowls and sprinkle with cheese, if desired.

☺ *Serving suggestion:* Serve with crisp bread sticks or crusty French rolls.

SOUTHWESTERN SMOKED TURKEY
AND BEAN PASTA

MAKES 4 SERVINGS

This high-fiber meal is also high in flavor and can be made as spicy as your family desires by using either mild, medium, or hot salsa. Rinse the beans, dice the turkey breast, and chop the cilantro while the pasta is cooking. The corn does not have to be thawed first.

> 2 14½-ounce cans chicken or vegetable broth
> 1 cup uncooked orzo pasta
> 1 15- or 16-ounce can black or kidney beans,
>   rinsed and drained
> 1 cup frozen corn kernels
> 1 cup (about 4 ounces) diced deli smoked turkey
>   breast or chopped cooked chicken
> ¾ cup chunky salsa
> 1 teaspoon ground cumin
> ¼ cup chopped cilantro
> 1 cup (4 ounces) shredded Monterey Jack or
>   cheddar cheese
> Sour cream (optional)

Bring broth to a boil, covered, in a large deep skillet over high heat. Add orzo and simmer, uncovered, for 7 minutes.

Stir in beans, corn, turkey, salsa, and cumin and return to a boil over high heat. Simmer for 3 minutes, stirring frequently. Stir in cilantro and ladle into shallow soup bowls. Top with cheese. Serve with sour cream, if desired.

🕑 *Serving suggestion:* Serve with tortilla chips or warm corn tortillas.

CHICKEN TORTELLINI TOSS WITH SUGAR SNAP PEAS

MAKES 4 SERVINGS

Skinless, boneless chicken thighs cut into 1-inch pieces may be substituted for the chicken tenders for a more economical dish.

    1 10-ounce package frozen sugar snap peas
    12 ounces chicken tenders
    1 tablespoon olive oil
    1 teaspoon bottled minced garlic
    1 14½-ounce can pasta-ready, diced tomatoes,
        undrained
    1 cup water
    ½ cup prepared pesto sauce
    1 9-ounce package refrigerated cheese tortellini
    Grated Parmesan cheese
    Freshly ground black pepper

Thaw sugar snap peas in a microwave oven on HIGH for about 3 minutes or in a colander under warm running water. Cut chicken into ¾-inch pieces.

Cook chicken in oil with garlic over medium-high heat for 3 minutes or until chicken is no longer pink, stirring once. Add tomatoes, water, and pesto and bring to a boil. Stir in tortellini and thawed peas. Cover and simmer for 10 minutes or until pasta is tender. Sprinkle with cheese and serve with pepper to taste.

Serving suggestion: Serve with crusty Italian or sourdough rolls.

Szechuan Chicken and Noodles

MAKES 4 SERVINGS

Prepared picante sauce adds a spicy note and gives wonderful flavor to this easy Oriental dish. Look for bottles of minced fresh gingerroot by the bottled minced garlic in the produce section of your supermarket. If it is not available, there is time to finely shred fresh gingerroot while the water comes to a boil.

6 cups very hot tap water
½ teaspoon salt
1 9-ounce package refrigerated fresh angel hair pasta
2 tablespoons soy sauce, divided
1 tablespoon Oriental sesame oil
12 ounces chicken tenders or chicken cut for stir-fry
2 teaspoons bottled minced gingerroot or finely shredded fresh gingerroot
1 teaspoon bottled minced garlic
1 tablespoon peanut or vegetable oil
1 cup diced red bell pepper
⅔ cup prepared picante sauce, preferably medium hot
2 tablespoons creamy peanut butter
3 scallions, cut diagonally into ½-inch pieces
⅓ cup chopped cashews or peanuts (optional)

Combine water and salt in a large deep skillet. Cover and bring to a boil over high heat. Add pasta and boil gently, uncovered, for 1 to 2 minutes or until hot, separating with a fork. (Do not overcook or pasta will be mushy.) Drain pasta and transfer to a large shallow bowl or pasta plate. Toss with 1 tablespoon soy sauce and the sesame oil. Cover with foil and set aside.

Meanwhile, combine chicken, remaining 1 tablespoon soy sauce, gingerroot, and garlic in a medium bowl. Dry the skillet and add peanut oil. Heat over medium-high heat. Add chicken mixture and stir-fry until chicken is no longer pink, about 3 minutes. Add bell pepper, picante sauce, and peanut butter. Reduce heat to medium and simmer for 3 minutes or until sauce thickens, stirring occasionally. Stir in scallions and spoon mixture over noodles. Sprinkle with nuts, if desired.

Serving suggestion: Serve with a cucumber salad.

ITALIAN-STYLE LINGUINI AND HAM SUPPER

MAKES 4 SERVINGS

This classic Italian olive oil and garlic sauce will enhance any of the many varieties of flavored pastas. Look for flavored linguini in the refrigerated pasta section of your supermarket or purchase fresh linguini by weight at Italian or gourmet food stores. Fresh garlic and cheese are a must for this recipe and may be prepared while the water comes to a boil and the pasta is cooking. For a meatless meal, omit the smoked ham.

3 quarts very hot tap water
1 teaspoon salt
1 9-ounce package refrigerated fresh linguini,
    preferably tomato-basil or herb flavor
2 cups cut fresh asparagus *or* 1 cup frozen peas
⅓ cup olive oil (preferably extra virgin)
1 tablespoon minced garlic
¼ cup canned chicken broth or reserved pasta
    cooking water
2 ounces sliced deli smoked ham, cut into short,
    thin strips
¾ cup (3 ounces) freshly grated Asiago,
    Parmesan, or Romano cheese
Freshly ground black pepper
2 tablespoons chopped fresh flat leaf parsley or
    basil (optional)

Combine water and salt in a large saucepan. Cover and bring to a boil over high heat. Add linguini and asparagus and boil, uncovered, for 2 minutes, stirring once. Pour pasta and asparagus into colander to drain. (Do not rinse.)

Heat oil and garlic in the same pot over medium-high heat. Cook for 1 minute or until the garlic begins to turn golden, but does not brown. Return pasta to pot and add broth and ham. Toss well to coat with the sauce. Arrange on four warmed dinner plates, top with cheese, and sprinkle with pepper to taste. Sprinkle with parsley, if desired.

Serving suggestion: Serve with crisp bread sticks.

CHEDDAR MAC AND HAM SUPPER

MAKES 4 SERVINGS

If you are using frozen broccoli florets, thaw them in the microwave on HIGH for 3 minutes and cut any large pieces in half. Get a ½-inch slice of ham at your deli counter and dice it while the pasta is cooking.

6 cups very hot tap water
¾ teaspoon salt, divided
7 ounces (2 cups) uncooked small pasta such as
  ditilini, small bow ties, shells, or elbows
2 cups small broccoli florets or 1 10-ounce
  package frozen, thawed
1 tablespoon all-purpose flour
1¼ cups half-and-half or milk
⅛ teaspoon cayenne pepper
1¼ cups (about 6 ounces) cubed deli smoked
  ham or honey cured ham
2 cups (8 ounces) shredded sharp cheddar cheese

Combine water and ½ teaspoon of salt in a large deep skillet. Cover and bring to a boil over high heat. Add pasta and boil gently, uncovered, for 5 minutes. Add broccoli to the skillet and continue boiling for 2 minutes or until pasta and broccoli are almost tender.

Meanwhile, place the flour in a small bowl. Gradually add half-and-half, mixing with a fork. Stir in remaining ¼ teaspoon salt and cayenne pepper. Transfer pasta and broccoli to colander to drain. (Do not rinse.) Place flour mixture in skillet and cook over medium heat for 1 minute, stirring frequently. Return pasta and broccoli to skillet and cook for 1 to 2 minutes or until sauce begins to thicken. Add ham to the skillet and heat through. Add cheese to the skillet and cook for 1 minute or until cheese melts and sauce thickens, stirring constantly.

🕐 *Serving suggestion:* Serve with a Caesar salad.

THAI CHICKEN PIZZA

MAKES 4 SERVINGS

Use kitchen shears or a large sharp chef's knife to cut this "fusion" pizza into wedges.

1 tablespoon vegetable oil
12 ounces chicken tenders or boneless chicken
   cut for stir-fry
1 teaspoon bottled minced garlic
1 teaspoon bottled minced fresh gingerroot *or*
   ½ teaspoon ground gingerroot
3 tablespoons bottled stir-fry sauce
¼ to ½ teaspoon dried hot red pepper flakes, as
   desired
2 scallions, sliced
1 12-inch prepared pizza crust or Italian bread
   shell
⅓ cup cocktail or dry roasted peanuts
⅓ cup coarsely chopped cilantro

Preheat oven to 450°F. Heat oil in large skillet over medium-high heat until hot. Add chicken, garlic, and gingerroot and stir-fry for 3 minutes. Add stir-fry sauce and pepper flakes and mix well. Remove from heat and stir in scallions. Spoon the mixture evenly over pizza crust and top with peanuts. Bake directly on oven rack for about 9 minutes or until crust is golden brown. Slide a cookie sheet under the hot pizza to remove from oven. Sprinkle with cilantro and cut into wedges.

🕒 *Serving suggestion:* Serve with a fresh fruit salad.

Classic Sausage and Mushroom Pizza

MAKES 4 SERVINGS

Nothing beats the flavor of an old-fashioned sausage pizza, otherwise known as Italian comfort food!

Purchase cleaned sliced mushrooms from the salad bar. If you purchase packaged sliced mushrooms rinse them quickly under cold water and pat dry with paper towels.

8 ounces uncooked Italian sausage, hot or mild as desired
2 cups (8 ounces) sliced fresh mushrooms
½ cup prepared pizza or marinara sauce
1 teaspoon dried basil
1 12-inch prepared pizza crust or Italian bread shell
2 cups (8 ounces) shredded mozzarella cheese

Preheat oven to 450°F. Squeeze the sausage from its casing into a large skillet. Cook over medium-high heat for 1 minute, breaking the sausage into pieces with a wooden spoon. Add mushrooms and cook for 4 to 5 minutes or until sausage is no longer pink. Pour off the drippings.

Meanwhile, combine pizza sauce and basil and spread evenly over pizza crust. Spoon sausage mixture over the sauce and top with cheese. Bake directly on oven rack for 9 to 10 minutes or until crust is golden brown and cheese is melted. Slide a cookie sheet under the hot pizza to remove it from the oven. Cut into wedges.

🕐 *Serving suggestion:* Serve with a tossed green salad with vinaigrette dressing.

Spinach and Three-Cheese Pizza

MAKES 4 SERVINGS

Purchase thinly sliced provolone cheese from the deli counter.

1 10-ounce package frozen chopped or leaf
  spinach
½ cup prepared pizza or marinara sauce
1 12-inch prepared pizza crust or Italian bread
  shell
1 teaspoon bottled minced garlic
¼ teaspoon dried hot red pepper flakes
4 ounces herbed feta or goat cheese, crumbled
¼ cup (1 ounce) grated Romano or Parmesan
  cheese
4 ounces thinly sliced provolone cheese

Preheat oven to 450°F. Thaw the spinach in a microwave oven on HIGH for about 3 minutes. Meanwhile, spread pizza sauce evenly over pizza crust. Squeeze as much liquid as possible from the thawed spinach. Arrange spinach over sauce and sprinkle with garlic and pepper flakes. Sprinkle feta and Romano cheese evenly over pizza and top with provolone cheese slices to cover. Bake directly on oven rack for about 9 minutes or until crust is golden. Slide a cookie sheet under the pizza to remove from the oven. Cut into wedges.

Serving suggestion: Serve with calamata olives and pepperoncini peppers.

MEDITERRANEAN-STYLE PIZZA

MAKES 4 SERVINGS

Placing the pizza directly on your oven rack will provide a crisp crust especially when you are using "wet" ingredients such as sliced tomatoes to top the pizza.

Look for sun-dried tomato pesto in the condiment section of specialty or gourmet food stores or some supermarkets. It will add a rich tomatoey flavor to the pizza, but if it is unavailable it may be omitted.

2 tablespoons sun-dried tomato pesto (optional)
1 12-inch prepared pizza crust or Italian bread shell
8 to 10 calamata or Spanish green olives, pitted, halved
2 large ripe tomatoes or 4 plum tomatoes, sliced thin
2 very thin slices large red onion, separated into rings
½ cup chopped, drained, bottled roasted red peppers (optional)
¼ teaspoon dried hot red pepper flakes
4 ounces feta or herbed feta cheese, crumbled
1 tablespoon garlic-infused or extra virgin olive oil
¼ cup packed fresh basil leaves

Preheat oven to 450°F. If desired, spread pesto lightly over pizza crust. Top with olives and tomatoes. Arrange red onion rings and, if desired, roasted peppers evenly over pizza. Sprinkle with pepper flakes, then cheese. Drizzle oil evenly over pizza. Bake directly on the oven rack for about 9 minutes or until crust is golden brown.

Meanwhile, cut the basil leaves into thin strips. Slide a cookie sheet under the pizza to remove from the oven. Sprinkle with basil and cut into wedges.

🕐 *Serving suggestion:* Serve with a marinated Greek or cucumber salad from the deli.

CARAMELIZED ONION AND SUN-DRIED TOMATO PIZZA

MAKES 4 SERVINGS

Sweet onion varieties such as Vadalia, Wala Wala, or Oso Sweet are available most of the year, but a yellow or red onion may be substituted.

 1 tablespoon olive oil
 1 tablespoon butter or margarine
 1 medium sweet onion, very thinly sliced
 Salt and freshly ground black pepper
 3 tablespoons prepared pesto sauce
 1 12-inch prepared pizza crust or Italian bread
   shell
 ¼ teaspoon dried hot red pepper flakes
 ⅓ cup coarsely chopped, drained, sun-dried
   tomatoes in oil
 4 ounces goat cheese or herbed goat cheese,
   crumbled
 ⅓ cup coarsely chopped walnuts or pine nuts

Preheat oven to 450°F. Heat oil and butter in a large skillet over medium-high heat. Add onion and cook for 6 to 7 minutes or until tender, stirring occasionally. Sprinkle lightly with salt and pepper.

Meanwhile, spread pesto evenly over pizza crust and top with pepper flakes. Arrange sun-dried tomatoes, cheese, and walnuts over pizza. Bake directly on oven rack for about 9 minutes or until crust is golden brown. Slide a cookie sheet under the hot pizza to remove from the oven. Cut into wedges.

🕐 *Serving suggestion:* Serve with a tossed green or Caesar salad.

5

Hot and Hearty Sandwiches

Serving sandwiches for dinner used to be considered a poor idea. We eat so many of them for lunch that they seem to be out of place at the dinner table. The recipes in this chapter command more respect. They are all interesting hot meals, substantial enough to satisfy the whole family at dinnertime.

Historically, the world has embraced the concept of the sandwich as the most complete form of meal satisfaction. Be it Greek, French, Italian, German, Mexican, or American, the sandwich fulfills many of our cravings. This chapter is a mix of ethnic recipes from *Beef and Bean Burritos, Italian Meatball Sandwiches, Greek-Style Pita Burgers, Old-World Bratwurst and Onion Sandwiches* to the all-American *Barbecued Beef Sandwiches with Cowboy Beans* and *Philly Cheesesteak Sandwiches*.

Lox and Scrambled Egg Sandwiches

MAKES 4 SERVINGS

For even quicker preparation, use cream cheese with chives and omit the sliced scallions.

> 6 eggs *or* 3 eggs plus 3 egg whites
> ¼ cup milk
> ¾ cup (3 ounces) lox or smoked salmon, cut into
>   short, thin strips
> ¼ cup thinly sliced scallions or chopped chives
> ¼ teaspoon salt
> ¼ teaspoon freshly ground black pepper
> 1 tablespoon butter or margarine
> 4 English muffins, split
> ⅓ cup light or regular cream cheese

Beat together eggs and milk. Stir in the lox, scallions, salt, and pepper. Melt butter in a large nonstick skillet over medium-high heat. Add egg mixture and cook for 3 to 4 minutes or until eggs are cooked to desired doneness, stirring occasionally.

Meanwhile, lightly toast the muffins and spread with cream cheese. Divide the egg mixture evenly over 4 muffin halves and top with remaining muffin halves.

🕐 *Serving suggestion:* Serve with cantaloupe wedges.

POACHED CHICKEN, HAM, AND ASPARAGUS SANDWICHES

MAKES 2 SERVINGS

This sandwich is served open-faced with a delicate cheese sauce.

¾ cup canned chicken broth *or* ½ cup broth
   plus ¼ cup dry vermouth
2 boneless, skinless chicken breast halves
¼ teaspoon salt
¼ teaspoon freshly ground black pepper
8 asparagus spears, trimmed to 5 inches in length
¼ cup milk or half-and-half
1 tablespoon all-purpose flour
2 slices Vienna or sourdough bread, toasted
2 slices smoked or honey cured deli ham
½ cup (2 ounces) shredded sharp cheddar cheese

Bring broth to a boil in a large skillet over high heat. Add chicken to skillet and sprinkle with salt and pepper. Cover and simmer for 4 minutes. Turn chicken and add asparagus to skillet. Cover and continue to simmer for 5 minutes or until chicken is cooked through and asparagus is crisp-tender.

While chicken is simmering, combine the milk and flour, mixing until smooth. Set aside. Place toast on serving plates and top with ham.

Remove chicken and asparagus from skillet with a slotted spoon or pancake turner, draining well. Place asparagus over ham and top with chicken.

Add the flour mixture to broth in skillet and cook for 1 minute, stirring constantly. Add cheese. Cook and stir until cheese melts and sauce is bubbly. Pour sauce evenly over chicken.

Serving suggestion: Serve with a tomato and basil salad.

PAN-GLAZED CHICKEN FOCACCIA SANDWICHES

MAKES 4 SERVINGS

Focaccia bread is an Italian flat bread made with olive oil and is often flavored with herbs and topped with onions or Parmesan cheese. If your supermarket has a bakery, ask them if they bake this type of bread. Focaccia freezes well and defrosts quickly. If it is not available, substitute 8 slices oval sourdough bread, toasted if desired.

> 4 4-ounce boneless, skinless chicken breast halves
> 1 tablespoon garlic or basil infused olive oil *or* 1 tablespoon olive oil plus ¼ teaspoon bottled minced garlic
> ½ teaspoon salt
> ¼ teaspoon freshly ground black pepper
> 2 tablespoons balsamic vinegar
> 1 tablespoon honey
> 1 10- to 12-ounce round loaf focaccia bread, about 8 inches in diameter
> Basil pesto, sun-dried tomato pesto, mayonnaise, or mustard as desired
> Spinach or romaine lettuce leaves

Place chicken between sheets of plastic wrap or waxed paper. Pound chicken to ½-inch thickness using a meat mallet or the bottom of a skillet or saucepan.

Heat oil in a large skillet over medium-high heat. Add chicken and sprinkle with salt and pepper. Cook for 5 minutes. Turn and continue to cook for 4 minutes. Combine vinegar and honey and add to the skillet. Continue to cook for 2 to 3 minutes or until chicken is cooked through and glazed, turning the chicken once.

Meanwhile, using a long serrated knife, cut bread crosswise into quarters. Split each quarter in half horizontally. Spread cut sides of bread lightly with pesto or other condiment(s) as desired. Layer spinach leaves over bottom of bread quarters, top with chicken, and drizzle with pan juices. Close sandwiches with remaining bread.

🕐 *Serving Suggestion:* Serve with a sliced ripe tomato and olive salad.

CHICKEN QUESADILLAS WITH CILANTRO CREAM

MAKES 4 LUNCHEON OR 2 DINNER SERVINGS

Quesadillas make a great planned meal for leftover chicken. Pick up a rotisserie chicken for dinner one night and reserve the leftovers for this easy, tasty meal the following night. Look for shredded Mexican blend cheese (a mix of four cheeses) in your supermarket's dairy case.

- 2 cups (8 ounces) shredded Mexican blend or Monterey Jack cheese
- 1 cup shredded or diced cooked chicken or deli smoked turkey breast
- ½ cup chunky salsa, divided
- ½ teaspoon bottled minced garlic
- 1 tablespoon butter or margarine, divided
- 2 10-inch flour tortillas
- ¼ cup light or regular sour cream
- ¼ cup coarsely chopped cilantro

Combine cheese, chicken, ¼ cup salsa, and garlic in a medium bowl. Melt ½ tablespoon butter in a 12-inch skillet or griddle over medium heat. Add one flour tortilla. Spoon the cheese mixture evenly over tortilla, leaving a ½-inch border. Top with remaining tortilla, pressing lightly. Cook for 5 to 6 minutes or until bottom tortilla is browned. Slide onto a plate. Melt the remaining ½ tablespoon butter in the skillet and invert quesadilla into skillet. Continue cooking for about 4 minutes or until bottom tortilla is browned.

Meanwhile, combine the remaining ¼ cup salsa, sour cream, and cilantro. Cut quesadilla into four wedges and serve with cilantro cream.

🕐 *Serving suggestion:* Serve with a sliced tomato and avocado salad.

TURKEY AND CRANBERRY FRENCH TOAST SANDWICHES

MAKES 2 SERVINGS

Look for cranberry chutney by the cranberry sauce or in the gourmet section of your supermarket.

> 4 ounces sliced deli turkey breast
> 4 ½-inch-thick slices Vienna or Italian bread
> 2 tablespoons cranberry chutney, cranberry
>   sauce, or cranberry relish
> 2 slices (2 ounces) provolone cheese
> 1 tablespoon butter or margarine
> 1 egg
> ½ cup milk
> Dash of nutmeg
> Sifted powdered sugar (optional)

Divide turkey over two slices of bread. Spread turkey with cranberry chutney. Top with cheese and close sandwiches with the remaining two slices of bread.

Melt butter in a large nonstick skillet over medium heat. Beat egg in a pie plate or large shallow bowl and beat in milk and nutmeg. Place one sandwich at a time in the egg mixture and let stand for 30 seconds per side. Cook in the melted butter for 3 to 4 minutes per side or until golden brown and cheese is melted. Sprinkle with powdered sugar, if desired.

☺ *Serving suggestion:* Serve with additional cranberry chutney for dipping.

CHICKEN MOLE BURRITOS

MAKES 4 SERVINGS

Look for mole paste (a spicy Mexican condiment made of ground chiles with a bit of unsweetened chocolate) in the ethnic section of your supermarket. One pound pork tenderloin cut into short, thin strips may be substituted for the chicken or turkey breast.

4 10-inch or 8 6-inch flour tortillas
1 tablespoon vegetable oil
1 cup chopped onion (frozen or fresh)
1 cup chopped red or green bell pepper
2 teaspoons bottled minced garlic
1 pound chicken or turkey breast cut for stir-fry
½ cup prepared mole paste
½ cup chicken or vegetable broth or water
½ cup light or regular sour cream
1 cup shredded lettuce
½ cup chopped tomato
Prepared salsa (optional)

Wrap tortillas in foil. Place in oven and turn the heat to 350°F. Bake for 12 to 15 minutes or until heated through.*

Meanwhile, heat the oil in a large skillet. Add the onion, bell pepper, and garlic and cook over medium-high heat for 3 minutes. Add chicken and cook for 5 minutes or until chicken is no longer pink. Reduce heat under skillet to medium-low. Add mole paste and broth and simmer, uncovered, for 5 minutes or until sauce thickens, stirring occasionally. (Additional broth or water may be added if sauce is too thick.)

*Tortillas may be heated in microwave oven if desired. Just before serving, stack tortillas and wrap loosely in waxed paper. Cook on HIGH for 1 minute or until heated through.

Spoon chicken mixture down center of warm tortillas and top with sour cream, lettuce, and tomato. Fold one end of tortilla over filling and roll up. Serve with salsa, if desired.

Serving suggestion: Serve with heated, canned refried beans mixed with a little salsa.

PHILLY CHEESESTEAK SANDWICHES

MAKES 2 SERVINGS

If you are thawing a frozen steak for this popular East Coast recipe, place in the refrigerator early in the day. A partially frozen steak will make thin slicing much easier.

1 tablespoon vegetable oil
½ medium onion, sliced thin
1 green bell pepper, cut into thin strips
½ pound well-trimmed boneless beef sirloin
   steak, cut into very thin slices
½ teaspoon salt
¼ teaspoon freshly ground black pepper
½ cup (4 ounces) shredded provolone or
   mozzarella cheese
2 hoagie or torpedo rolls, split

Heat oil in a large skillet over medium-high heat. Add onion and bell pepper and cook for 4 to 5 minutes or until vegetables are crisp-tender, stirring occasionally. Add steak and sprinkle with salt and pepper. Stir-fry for 2 to 3 minutes or until meat is still pink in the center (do not overcook). Sprinkle cheese over meat mixture and turn off heat. Spoon mixture into rolls.

🕐 *Serving suggestion:* Serve with a marinated vegetable salad.

Italian Meatball Sandwiches

MAKES 4 SERVINGS

These meatballs brown quickly over medium-high heat. To turn them often simply shake the skillet from time to time until they are browned on all sides.

> 1 pound lean ground beef
> 1 tablespoon dehydrated onion
> 1 teaspoon bottled minced garlic
> 1 teaspoon dried basil
> ½ teaspoon salt
> 1½ cups prepared spaghetti sauce with
>   mushrooms
> 4 hoagie or torpedo rolls, split, toasted if desired
> 1 cup (4 ounces) shredded mozzarella cheese

Combine ground beef, onion, garlic, basil, and salt, mixing lightly but thoroughly. Shape to form 16 meatballs, about 1½ inches in diameter. Brown meatballs in a large deep nonstick skillet over medium-high heat for about 8 minutes, turning occasionally.

Reduce heat and add spaghetti sauce. Cover and simmer for about 6 minutes or until sauce is hot and meatballs are cooked through. Transfer four meatballs to each roll. Spoon sauce over meatballs and sprinkle with cheese.

Serving suggestion: Serve with pepperoncini peppers.

GRILLED BEEF FAJITAS

MAKES 4 SERVINGS

The reigning "king" of Southwestern fare, this classic sandwich combines delicious tastes and textures all rolled into a flour tortilla.

½ cup salsa or picante sauce plus additional for
   serving
1 tablespoon fresh lime juice
1 tablespoon vegetable oil
2 cloves garlic, minced, *or* 1 teaspoon bottled
   minced garlic
1 teaspoon ground cumin
8 6- to 7-inch flour tortillas
1 well-trimmed boneless beef top sirloin steak,
   cut 1 inch thick
½ teaspoon salt
1 green bell pepper
1 red or yellow bell pepper
4 ¼-inch-thick slices red or yellow onion
Sour cream (optional)

Prepare charcoal or gas grill. Combine salsa, lime juice, oil, garlic, and cumin in a small bowl and set aside. Wrap tortillas in heavy-duty aluminum foil. Sprinkle steak with salt. Cut bell peppers in half lengthwise, discarding stems and seeds.

Place steak, onion slices, and peppers on grill over medium-hot coals. Place tortilla packet on outer edge of grill. Brush half of salsa mixture over steak, onion slices, and peppers, cover, and grill for 5 minutes. Turn steak, onion slices, peppers, and tortilla packet. Brush remaining salsa mixture over steak, onion slices, and peppers. Continue grilling, covered, for 4 to 5 minutes or until steak is medium rare and onion slices and peppers are crisp-tender. Transfer steak and peppers to carving board. Thinly slice steak and peppers and separate onion slices into rings. Arrange steak and vegetables in warm tortillas. Fold one end of tortilla over filling and roll up. Serve with additional salsa and sour cream, if desired.

Serving suggestion: Serve with heated, drained, canned pinto beans topped with shredded Monterey Jack cheese.

BEEF AND BEAN BURRITOS

MAKES 4 SERVINGS

Look for frozen chopped onions in the freezer section by the frozen potatoes or use chopped onions from the supermarket salad bar. Chihuahua is an authentic crumbling cheese from Mexico. If it is not available, substitute packaged shredded Mexican cheese, which is a blend of four cheeses, or shredded Monterey Jack cheese.

> 4 10-inch or 8 6-inch flour tortillas
> ½ pound lean ground beef or turkey
> 1 teaspoon garlic salt
> 1 teaspoon ground cumin
> ¼ teaspoon cinnamon (optional)
> 1 cup frozen chopped onion
> 1 small red or green bell pepper
> 1 16-ounce can pinto or kidney beans, drained
> 1 cup prepared salsa or picante sauce
> ¼ cup chopped cilantro (optional)
> 1 cup (4 ounces) crumbled Chihuahua cheese

Wrap tortillas in foil. Place in oven and turn heat to 350°F. Bake for 12 to 15 minutes or until heated through.*

Meanwhile, place ground beef in a large skillet and sprinkle with garlic salt, cumin, and, if desired, cinnamon. Cook over medium heat for 1 minute, breaking up ground beef with a wooden spoon. Stir in

---

Tortillas may be heated in the microwave oven, if desired. Just before serving, stack tortillas and wrap loosely in waxed paper. Cook on HIGH for 1 minute or until heated through.

onion and continue cooking for 2 minutes. Meanwhile, chop the bell pepper and stir it into the ground beef mixture. When ground beef is no longer pink, stir in beans and salsa. Simmer for 6 to 8 minutes, stirring occasionally.

Stir in cilantro, if desired. Spoon mixture down center of warmed tortillas and sprinkle with cheese. Fold one end of tortilla over filling and roll up.

Serving suggestion: Serve with sour cream and diced ripe avocado.

BEST-EVER CHEESEBURGERS

MAKES 4 SERVINGS

Everyone has their favorite hamburger or cheeseburger: here's mine. The National Cattlemen's Beef Association recommends cooking ground beef to 160°F or until no longer pink in center. To quickly peel the onion, cut the slices first and then peel off the outer layer. Wrap and refrigerate the ends of the onion to dice and use another day.

1¼ pounds ground beef chuck
⅓ cup ketchup or prepared chili sauce
2 tablespoons seasoned or plain dry bread crumbs
1 egg or egg white
1 tablespoon dehydrated minced onion flakes
½ teaspoon garlic salt
¼ teaspoon freshly ground black pepper
4 ¼-inch slices large red or sweet onion
Olive oil (optional)
4 1-ounce slices cheddar or Monterey Jack cheese
4 whole-wheat or bakery-style hamburger buns,
    split, toasted or grilled if desired
4 romaine or red leaf lettuce leaves
4 slices large ripe tomato
Condiments (optional)

Prepare gas or charcoal grill or preheat broiler. In a medium bowl, combine ground beef, ketchup, bread crumbs, egg, onion flakes, garlic salt, and pepper, mixing lightly but thoroughly. Shape to form four ½-inch-thick patties. If desired, lightly brush onion slices with oil. Place patties and onion slices on the grill over medium-hot coals or on the rack of a broiler pan. Grill or broil 4 to 5 inches from the heat source for about 10 minutes or until centers of burgers are no longer pink, turning burgers and onion slices after 5 minutes of cooking. Top burgers with cheese during the last 1 minute of cooking. Serve burgers in buns with lettuce and tomato. Serve with mustard, mayonnaise, or ketchup as desired.

Serving suggestion: Serve with dill pickle spears, calamata olives, and pepperoncini peppers.

BARBECUED BEEF SANDWICHES WITH COWBOY BEANS

Cumin gives the pinto beans their Western flavor! To quickly drain the can of beans, open the can and, holding the lid in place, drain the liquid into the sink. (No need to wash a colander or strainer!)

It is important to purchase rare roast beef so that it will not overcook in the sauce. The beans pick up the spicy flavor of the barbecue sauce left in the pan. For an extra spicy version, increase the hot pepper sauce to ¼ teaspoon.

> ¾ cup ketchup
> ⅓ cup packed light brown sugar
> 2 tablespoons Worcestershire sauce
> 1 tablespoon yellow or Dijon mustard
> ⅛ teaspoon hot pepper sauce
> 1 pound thinly sliced rare deli roast beef
> 4 submarine sandwich rolls or hoagie rolls, split,
>   lightly toasted
> 1 16-ounce can pinto beans, drained
> 1 teaspoon ground cumin

Combine ketchup, brown sugar, Worcestershire sauce, mustard, and hot sauce in a large deep skillet. Cook over medium heat until sugar melts and sauce simmers, stirring frequently. Separate slices of beef and add to skillet one at a time, turning to coat with sauce and pushing to the edge of the skillet. When all slices are added, simmer for 2 minutes or until hot, turning often.

With tongs, transfer beef to rolls, leaving some of the barbecue sauce in the pan. Add beans and cumin and simmer, uncovered, for 3 to 4 minutes or until heated through, stirring occasionally. Serve beans alongside sandwiches.

Serving suggestion: Serve with a shredded carrot salad or a cucumber salad.

CLASSIC REUBEN SANDWICHES

MAKES 4 SERVINGS

Try this quick version of America's favorite deli sandwich.

12 ounces sliced deli corned beef
4 slices rye or pumpernickel bread, toasted
¼ cup light or regular mayonnaise
2 tablespoons chili sauce or ketchup
1 teaspoon drained bottled horseradish
½ cup well-drained sauerkraut
4 slices (4 ounces) Swiss cheese

Preheat broiler. Arrange corned beef over toast. Combine mayonnaise, chili sauce, and horseradish. Spread half of mixture over corned beef and top with sauerkraut. Spread remaining mayonnaise mixture over sauerkraut and top with cheese. Place sandwiches on foil-lined baking sheet or broiler pan. Broil 5 inches from heat for 5 to 6 minutes or until cheese is melted and sandwiches are hot.

Serving suggestion: Serve with dill pickle spears.

GREEK-STYLE PITA BURGERS

MAKES 4 SERVINGS

This burger has the authentic flavor of a gyro sandwich. To quickly warm pita bread, stack and wrap loosely in plastic wrap or waxed paper. Heat in microwave oven on HIGH for 1 minute.

> 1¼ pounds lean ground lamb or beef
> 1 tablespoon plus 1 teaspoon dehydrated minced
>   onion flakes, divided
> 1¼ teaspoons bottled minced garlic, divided
> ½ teaspoon salt
> ¼ teaspoon freshly ground black pepper
> ½ cup plain low-fat yogurt
> ½ cup chopped unpeeled cucumber
> 1 teaspoon dried mint or oregano leaves
> 4 pita pocket breads, warmed if desired
> 4 leaves romaine lettuce
> 4 large slices tomato

Prepare gas or charcoal grill or preheat broiler. In a medium bowl, combine meat, 1 tablespoon onion, 1 teaspoon garlic, salt, and pepper, mixing lightly but thoroughly. Shape to form four ½-inch-thick patties. Place patties on grill over medium-hot coals or on rack of broiler pan. Grill or broil 4 to 5 inches from heat source, for 10 to 12 minutes or until center of burgers are no longer pink, turning once.

Meanwhile, combine yogurt, cucumber, mint, remaining 1 teaspoon onion and ¼ teaspoon garlic and mix well. Cut tops off of pita bread and open into pockets. Fill each pocket with lettuce, tomato, and a meat pattie. Top with yogurt mixture.

Serving suggestion: Serve with calamata olives.

SAUSAGE AND PEPPERS SANDWICHES

MAKES 4 SERVINGS

You may feel free to substitute any fully cooked sausages for the kielbasa. Some specialty markets carry chicken Italian sausages in packets of four that work very well in this recipe.

> 1 to 1¼ pounds fully cooked kielbasa or Polish
>   sausage
> 1 small (or ½ large) red bell pepper
> 1 small (or ½ large) green or yellow bell pepper
> ½ medium red or yellow onion
> ½ cup prepared spaghetti sauce or pizza sauce
> 4 submarine or hoagie rolls, split, toasted if
>   desired

Cut sausage into four pieces and cook in a large deep nonstick skillet over medium-high heat for 4 minutes, turning once. Meanwhile, cut the bell peppers into thin strips and the onion into thin wedges. Add pepper strips and onion wedges to the skillet. Cover and cook over medium-low heat for 10 minutes or until vegetables are crisp-tender and sausages are well browned, turning the sausages and stirring the pepper mixture once. Add spaghetti sauce. Turn heat to high and cook for 1 minute, stirring constantly, or until sauce is very hot. Serve sausages, vegetables, and sauce in rolls.

Serving suggestion: Serve with applesauce or a fruit salad.

OLD-WORLD BRATWURST AND ONION SANDWICHES

MAKES 4 SERVINGS

If you are lucky enough to have a German or international deli in your area, purchase their freshly made bratwurst for this tasty sandwich.

2 teaspoons butter or margarine
1 large onion, sliced thin
4 fully cooked bratwurst sausages, about 1 pound
½ cup beer (not dark beer)
4 onion frankfurter or hoagie rolls, split, toasted if desired
¾ cup well-drained sauerkraut (optional)
Dusseldorf or coarse-grained mustard

Melt butter in a large skillet over medium-high heat. Add onion and cook for 2 minutes or until onion is wilted, stirring occasionally. Add bratwurst and beer and bring to a boil. Cover, reduce heat, and simmer for 5 minutes.

Uncover and continue cooking until liquid evaporates, about 2 minutes. Continue cooking, uncovered, for 3 minutes or until bratwurst and onion are browned, turning bratwurst and stirring onion occasionally. Serve bratwurst in rolls and top with onion. Top with sauerkraut if desired. Serve with mustard.

🕐 *Serving suggestion:* Serve with shoestring potatoes or chips.

PORTABELLO AND EGGPLANT PARMESAN SANDWICHES

MAKES 4 SERVINGS

Look for packages of portabello mushroom caps in your supermarket's produce section.

> 4 portabello mushroom caps, each about 4 inches
>   in diameter
> 4 ½-inch-thick slices large eggplant
> ½ cup bottled light or regular Caesar or Italian
>   salad dressing, divided
> ⅓ cup prepared marinara sauce or pizza sauce
> 4 round slices provolone cheese (4 ounces)
> 8 slices sourdough bread *or* 4 kaiser rolls, split,
>   lightly toasted if desired

Preheat broiler. Place mushrooms and eggplant slices on rack of broiler pan. Brush evenly with ¼ cup dressing. Broil 3 to 4 inches from heat source for 5 minutes. Turn and brush with remaining dressing. Continue to broil for 4 minutes or until vegetables are tender. Remove mushrooms and set aside. Spread marinara sauce evenly over eggplant slices and top with cheese. Broil for 1 to 2 minutes or until cheese is melted. (If desired, slip off and discard the eggplant skin.) Place mushroom caps and eggplant slices between bread.

Serving suggestion: Serve with a tossed green salad.

6

Main Dish Salads

No longer do salads need to be boring combinations of lettuce, tomato, and an occasional cucumber! Nor must they be relegated to the supporting cast of the evening meal. Today, trendy and even traditional restaurants have paved the way for exciting salads to become the rising stars of their dinner menus by using every type of seafood, poultry, or meat and grains and legumes like couscous and white beans. Americans can't seem to get enough of the popular textural and temperature combinations of hot ingredients served on cold greens.

This chapter showcases traditional favorites such as *Classic Niçoise Salad* and also introduces new salad ideas such as *Grilled Chicken and White Bean Salad* and *Warm Goat Cheese Salad*.

Classic Niçoise Salad

This delicious salad is traditionally served at room temperature in cafés and brasseries throughout France. The dressing is a traditional blend of French ingredients, but if you would rather substitute a prepared dressing to save even more time, stir ½ teaspoon dried crushed tarragon into ⅓ cup light or regular Caesar salad dressing.

½ pound small red potatoes
¼ pound fresh green beans, stems trimmed
1 egg (optional)
3 tablespoons light or regular mayonnaise
2 tablespoons extra virgin olive oil
1 tablespoon Dijon mustard
½ teaspoon dried tarragon, crushed
¼ teaspoon salt
¼ teaspoon freshly ground black pepper
6 cups (8 ounces) packed torn romaine lettuce or
    mixed bitter salad greens
1 large ripe tomato or 2 plum tomatoes, cut into
    thin wedges
16 niçoise or calamata olives
1 6½-ounce can white tuna in water, drained
Garlic croutons (optional)

Scrub the potatoes but do not dry them. Place wet potatoes in 8-inch square glass baking dish or microwave casserole. Cover with vented plastic wrap. Microwave on HIGH for 3 minutes. Wash green beans, trim ends, and cut in half if very long. Add beans to potatoes in baking dish and cover with vented plastic wrap. Continue to microwave on HIGH for 4 to 5 minutes or until vegetables are tender. Transfer to sink and fill dish with cold water. Drain water and fill again with cold water to stop cooking and cool the vegetables. Let stand while preparing salad.

If desired, crack egg into a small custard cup. Cover with vented plastic wrap. Microwave at 50 percent power for 1 to 1½ minutes or until egg is opaque. Let stand for 1 minute. Slip egg into cold water with potatoes and green beans to stop cooking.

Combine mayonnaise, oil, mustard, tarragon, salt, and pepper in a small bowl, mixing with a fork or wire whisk until well blended.

Arrange lettuce on serving plates. Arrange tomato and olives attractively around edges of salads. Break tuna into chunks and arrange over lettuce. Drain potatoes, cut into quarters, and arrange around edges of salads. Drain green beans and arrange over salad. Drain and coarsely chop egg and arrange over salads. Drizzle dressing evenly over salads. If desired, top with croutons and serve with additional freshly ground black pepper.

Serving suggestion: Serve with warm French bread baguettes and garlic or basil infused olive oil for dipping.

SPICY CRAB CAKES ON BITTER GREENS

MAKES 4 SERVINGS

To easily crush saltines or oyster crackers place in a plastic bag and lightly pound with your fist or a meat mallet until coarsely crushed.

½ pound lump crabmeat *or* 2 6-ounce cans
    crabmeat, well-drained
½ cup coarsely crushed saltines or oyster crackers
¼ cup plus 2 tablespoons light or regular
    mayonnaise, divided
1 egg
½ teaspoon hot pepper sauce
1 tablespoon vegetable oil
6 cups (8 ounces) packed mixed bitter salad
    greens
¼ cup light or regular Caesar or Italian salad
    dressing
2 teaspoons Dijon mustard
Lemon wedges for garnish

Combine crabmeat, cracker crumbs, ¼ cup mayonnaise, egg, and hot pepper sauce, mixing well. Heat oil in a large nonstick skillet over medium-high heat until hot. Shape crab mixture into four patties about ½ inch thick. Cook in hot oil for 2 to 3 minutes per side or until golden brown.

Meanwhile, toss greens with dressing and transfer to four serving plates. Combine the remaining 2 tablespoons of mayonnaise with mustard and mix well. Arrange crab cakes over greens and spoon mustard mixture over crab cakes. Serve with lemon wedges.

Serving suggestion: Serve with sourdough bread.

LATIN-STYLE LOBSTER VEGETABLE SALAD

MAKES 4 SERVINGS

If you are lucky enough to live in an area where fresh lobster is abundant and reasonably priced try this flavorful salad for a romantic summer dinner. If you are not so lucky, don't fret. Imitation lobster (made from Alaskan pollock fish fillets) is a good substitute at a very reasonable price.

> 1 cup frozen corn kernels
> 6 cups (8 ounces) packed mixed bitter salad
>   greens
> 8 ounces cooked lobster meat or imitation lobster
>   meat cut into ¾-inch pieces (about 1½ cups)
> 1 15-ounce can black beans, rinsed and drained
> 1 large tomato, seeded and diced
> ¼ cup coarsely chopped cilantro
> ⅓ cup garlic infused or extra virgin olive oil
> 3 tablespoons fresh lime juice
> ¾ teaspoon ground coriander
> ¾ teaspoon bottled minced jalapeño peppers *or*
>   ¼ teaspoon hot pepper sauce
> ½ teaspoon ground cumin
> ¼ teaspoon salt
> Lime wedges (optional)

Rinse corn under cool water until thawed. Arrange salad greens on four serving plates and top with lobster, drained corn, beans, tomato, and cilantro. Combine oil, lime juice, coriander, jalapeño peppers, cumin, and salt, mixing with a fork or small wire whisk until well blended. Drizzle mixture evenly over salads and serve with lime wedges, if desired.

Serving suggestion: Serve with warm corn or flour tortillas.

Composed Salad of Rotisserie Chicken, Pear, and Walnuts with Garlic Toasts

MAKES 4 SERVINGS

This is a wonderful salad to serve during the warm days of Indian summer when pears are at their peak. Red Bartletts make a very attractive salad. If you have an apple slicer and corer (a round metal spokelike gadget) use it to make quick work of coring and slicing the pear. If pears are not in season, substitute an Asian pear, a crisp and juicy cross between a pear and an apple.

Many supermarkets now make their own versions of rotisserie roasted chicken. If that is unavailable, however, you may substitute any leftover cooked chicken or turkey. If you have just returned from the market and the chicken is still warm, it will provide a wonderful temperature contrast to the chilled greens, but the chicken may be served cold or at room temperature as well.

½ cup walnut pieces

¼ cup plus 1 tablespoon garlic-infused olive oil *or* 1 tablespoon olive oil plus ½ teaspoon bottled minced garlic, divided

12 ½-inch-thick slices French bread baguette

6 cups packed mixed bitter salad greens

12 ounces sliced or shredded seasoned rotisserie chicken

1 ripe pear, cored, sliced

4 to 6 ounces Gorgonzola or Stilton cheese, crumbled (optional)

2 tablespoons balsamic vinegar

¼ teaspoon salt

Freshly ground black pepper

Preheat oven to 425°F. Place walnuts on a baking sheet and place in oven to toast for 5 minutes while oven is heating to 425°F. Meanwhile, brush 1 tablespoon oil evenly over both sides of bread slices. Transfer toasted walnuts to a paper towel and set aside to cool. Place bread slices on same baking sheet and toast in oven for 8 minutes or until crisp and golden brown, turning after 4 minutes.

Meanwhile, arrange salad greens on four dinner plates. Arrange chicken, pear, and, if desired, cheese over greens. Rub toasted walnuts in paper towel to remove any bitter skins and arrange walnuts over salad. Combine remaining ¼ cup oil with vinegar and salt, mixing well with a fork or small wire whisk. Drizzle dressing evenly over salad and serve with garlic toasts and pepper.

Serving suggestion: Serve with sugar cookies for dessert.

GRILLED CHICKEN AND
WHITE BEAN SALAD

MAKES 4 SERVINGS

This room temperature salad is inspired by the cuisine of Tuscany, Italy.

4 ½-inch-thick slices Italian or Vienna bread
6 tablespoons light or regular Caesar or Italian
    salad dressing, divided
½ teaspoon dried rosemary, crushed
4 4-ounce boneless, skinless chicken breast halves
3 cups packed torn spinach leaves
1 16- or 19-ounce can cannellini beans or great
    northern beans, rinsed and drained
1 large ripe tomato or 2 plum tomatoes, diced
2 tablespoons finely diced red onion
Freshly ground black pepper

Prepare charcoal or gas grill or preheat broiler. Brush both sides of bread lightly with 1 tablespoon dressing. Combine 2 tablespoons dressing and rosemary and brush over both sides of chicken. Grill or broil chicken 4 to 5 inches from the heat source for 6 minutes. Turn chicken and continue grilling or broiling for 5 to 6 minutes or until chicken is cooked through, adding bread during last several minutes of cooking time and turning once to toast on both sides.

Meanwhile, arrange spinach on four serving plates. Combine beans, tomato, and red onion with remaining 3 tablespoons of dressing. Arrange over spinach. Cut toasted bread into ¾-inch squares and sprinkle over bean mixture. Top with chicken and serve with pepper.

Serving suggestion: Serve with calamata or niçoise olives and pepperoncini peppers.

PICANTE CHICKEN SALAD

MAKES 4 SERVINGS

This tasty salad gets its zing from the ever popular pantry ingredient, picante sauce. Bottled or refrigerated salsa will work just as well.

1 tablespoon garlic-infused olive oil *or*
    1 tablespoon olive oil plus ½ teaspoon bottled
    minced garlic
12 ounces chicken or turkey breast cut for stir-fry
5 tablespoons prepared picante sauce, divided
6 cups (8 ounces) packed torn assorted salad
    greens
1 cup prepared garlic croutons
16 red or yellow cherry tomatoes, halved if large
¼ cup light or regular Caesar or ranch salad
    dressing

Heat oil in a large nonstick skillet over medium-high heat. Stir-fry chicken strips in hot oil for 3 to 4 minutes or until chicken is cooked through. Add 3 tablespoons picante sauce and heat through, tossing well. Remove from heat and set aside.

Combine salad greens, croutons, and tomatoes in a large bowl. Add salad dressing and the remaining 2 tablespoons of picante sauce. Toss salad. Arrange on four dinner plates and top with chicken mixture.

🕐 *Serving suggestion:* Serve with warm dinner rolls.

ORIENTAL CHICKEN SALAD

MAKES 4 SERVINGS

This salad is perfect for leftover rotisserie chicken or even barbecued chicken without the skin. Look for packages of shredded carrots and bottles of minced fresh gingerroot in the produce section of your supermarket when you are purchasing prewashed packaged spinach and salad greens. Seasoned rice vinegar, Oriental sesame oil, and hot chili oil may be found in the ethnic section of your supermarket.

3 cups packed torn spinach leaves
3 cups packed torn salad greens
1½ cups shredded cooked chicken or diced deli
  turkey breast
1 cup fresh bean sprouts
½ cup canned, drained, sliced water chestnuts or
  bamboo shoots
½ cup coarsely shredded carrots
3 tablespoons seasoned rice vinegar or white wine
  vinegar
2 tablespoons soy sauce
1 tablespoon Oriental sesame oil
1 teaspoon honey
½ teaspoon bottled minced fresh gingerroot or
  ground gingerroot
¼ to ½ teaspoon hot chili oil (optional)
Chopped roasted peanuts or cashews

Combine spinach, lettuce, chicken, bean sprouts, water chestnuts, and carrots in a large bowl. Combine vinegar, soy sauce, sesame oil, honey, gingerroot, and, if desired, hot chili oil, mixing well in a small bowl. Drizzle over lettuce mixture and toss well. Transfer to four serving plates and sprinkle with peanuts.

Serving suggestion: Serve with Oriental pita crisps (cut triangles from pita pocket breads, brush lightly with Oriental sesame oil, and toast or broil until crisp).

ROAST BEEF AND BLUE CHEESE SALAD WITH GARLIC-HERB MUFFINS

MAKES 4 SERVINGS

This delicious and hearty salad is easily halved to serve two. Look for packages of prewashed spinach and salad greens in your supermarket produce section.

> 2 English muffins, split
> 2 tablespoons butter
> ¼ teaspoon dried basil
> ¼ teaspoon dried thyme leaves
> 1 clove garlic, minced, *or* ½ teaspoon bottled minced garlic
> 4 cups packed torn assorted salad greens
> 4 cups packed torn spinach leaves
> ⅓ cup bottled light or regular Caesar salad dressing
> 8 ounces rare deli roast beef, cut ¼ inch thick
> 2 ripe tomatoes, cut into wedges
> ½ cup (2 ounces) crumbled Roquefort, blue, or Gorgonzola cheese
> Freshly ground black pepper

Preheat broiler. Place muffins cut-side up on baking sheet or broiler pan. Place butter in a small microwave-safe bowl or custard cup. Cook in a microwave on HIGH for 20 seconds to soften. Add basil, thyme, and garlic to softened butter and mix well. Spread evenly over muffins. Broil 3 to 4 inches from the heat source for about 2 minutes or until lightly toasted.

Combine salad greens and spinach in a large bowl. Add dressing and toss lightly. Arrange greens on four serving plates. Cut roast beef into 1″ × ¼″ × ¼″ strips. Arrange roast beef and tomatoes attractively over greens and sprinkle with cheese. Sprinkle with pepper to taste. Serve with muffins.

🕐 *Serving suggestion:* Serve a fruit sorbet or frozen yogurt with fresh fruit for dessert.

WILTED SPINACH SALAD WITH BACON AND SCALLOPS

MAKES 4 SERVINGS

Look for packages of prewashed spinach in your supermarket produce section or purchase about 8 ounces from the salad bar. Purchase apple wood smoked bacon for a very robust flavor that compliments the sweetness of the scallops.

3 thick or 4 regular slices bacon, preferably apple
  wood smoked
1 pound sea scallops or bay scallops
1 teaspoon Hungarian sweet paprika
½ teaspoon salt
¼ teaspoon freshly ground black pepper
6 cups packed spinach leaves, stems removed
¼ cup finely chopped shallots or onion
1 teaspoon bottled minced garlic
¼ cup red wine vinegar
1 teaspoon sugar
¼ teaspoon dry mustard
1 cup herb or garlic croutons
Lemon wedges (optional)

Cut bacon crosswise into ¼-inch strips. Cook bacon in a large skillet over medium-high heat until crisp, stirring occasionally. Using a slotted spoon or spatula, transfer bacon to a paper towel to drain.

Meanwhile, rinse the scallops in cold water and pat dry with paper towel. Add to hot bacon drippings in pan and sprinkle with paprika, salt, and pepper. Cook until opaque, about 6 minutes for sea scallops or 4 minutes for bay scallops, turning once.

Meanwhile, arrange spinach on four serving plates. Using a slotted spoon or spatula, arrange scallops over spinach. Add shallots and garlic to pan drippings and cook for 1 minute. Add vinegar, sugar, and mustard and bring to a boil, stirring constantly. Pour over scallops and spinach and sprinkle with reserved bacon and croutons. Serve with lemon wedges, if desired.

🕐 *Serving suggestion:* Serve with crusty rye rolls.

Warm Goat Cheese Salad

MAKES 4 SERVINGS

Look for mixed bitter salad greens (sometimes called mesclun mix or gourmet salad greens) in your supermarket produce section or substitute a combination of torn red leaf and romaine lettuce.

> 1 8-ounce log or 2 4-ounce logs goat cheese
> (chèvre) or herbed goat cheese
> ½ cup fresh French or Italian bread crumbs
> ½ teaspoon dried thyme leaves
> ¼ cup plus 2 tablespoons extra virgin olive oil,
> divided
> 2 garlic cloves, halved, peeled
> 2 tablespoons white or regular balsamic vinegar
> ¼ teaspoon salt
> ¼ teaspoon freshly ground black pepper
> 8 cups (10 ounces) packed mixed bitter salad
> greens
> 3 bottled roasted red peppers, well drained, cut
> into strips

Cut cheese crosswise into 8 slices. Combine bread crumbs and thyme in a shallow dish. Brush cheese slices with 1 tablespoon olive oil and roll in crumbs, patting well to coat. Heat 1 tablespoon olive oil in a large nonstick skillet over medium heat. Add garlic cloves and cheese slices. Cook for 3 to 4 minutes per side or until bread crumbs are golden brown and cheese is warmed but not melted.

Meanwhile, combine the remaining ¼ cup olive oil, vinegar, salt, and pepper, mixing well with a fork or small wire whisk. Combine salad greens and roasted peppers in a large bowl. Add olive oil mixture and toss to coat. Arrange salad on four dinner plates and top with warm cheese (discard oil and garlic cloves in pan). Serve with additional pepper, if desired.

Serving suggestion: Serve with crusty French bread or whole-grain rolls.

Warm Couscous Vegetable Salad

MAKES 3 TO 4 SERVINGS:

For an interesting appearance, use a cheese planer or small sharp knife to "shave" a wedge of Parmesan or Asiago cheese into paper thin slices. Use a mixture of colorful bell peppers from the salad bar to add sweetness and color to this tasty salad.

¼ cup olive oil, divided
1 cup diced red or yellow bell pepper or a
    combination
½ cup chopped yellow or red onion
1 cup (4 ounces) sliced crimini or button
    mushrooms or halved oyster mushrooms
1 teaspoon bottled minced garlic
1 14½-ounce can vegetable broth
1 cup uncooked couscous
¼ teaspoon salt
¼ teaspoon freshly ground black pepper
1 cup coarsely chopped tomato
¼ cup chopped fresh basil or parsley
2 tablespoons balsamic vinegar or fresh lemon
    juice
Fresh spinach leaves (optional)
¼ cup (1 ounce) shaved or grated Parmesan or
    Asiago cheese

Heat 2 tablespoons oil in a large deep skillet over medium-high heat. Add bell peppers and onion and cook for 2 minutes, stirring occasionally. Add mushrooms and garlic and reduce heat to medium. Cook for 1 minute.

Stir in broth and bring to a boil. Stir in couscous, salt, and pepper. Cover, turn off heat, and let stand for 5 minutes or until liquid is absorbed. Stir in tomato, basil, remaining 2 tablespoons oil, and vinegar. Mix well. Serve salad on a bed of spinach leaves, if desired. Top with cheese.

☺ *Serving suggestion:* Serve with bagel or pita chips.

Index

INDEX